Detroit Fire
Historical Record

1825 - 1977

Cover dedicated to Raymond Vallad who wore badge 600 from Feb. 1917 to Dec. 30, 1958

1

Detroit Firemen's Memorial – Mt. Elliott Cemetery

FOR
FIRE

John Miller	Timothy F. O'Shea	William M. Burgess	Stanley Thornton
James H. O'Grady	Otto Habermas	George F. Pokraefke	Werner Blaess
Michael McQueen	William Huffman	Frank J. Riopel	Ellsworth Carroll
Richard Filban	William J. Moran	James J. Templeton	Dwight Higinbotham
James J. Powers	William J.	Stanley T. Hanley	Nicholas Konen
David M. Clark	Otto A. Maffice	George A. Merrill	Bruno Koluch
Patrick J. Coughlin	Oscar Locke	Anthony Brosowski	Stephen Szpunar
Peter C. Schwartz	Alexander Cockburn	Luther Adam	Albert Booth
Hugh Garrity	Alonzo F. Raymond	Louis A. Pape	Jack J. Campell
David Boyd	Richard Beard	Chester G. Simcox	Chester R. Beals
Henry M. Turner	Stanley Dopris	Russell M. Kelly	Jack Trim
Octavious G. Robinson	William O'Brien	Shirley R. Colburne	Lyle W. Ingram
Eugene M. McCarthy	James Gendry	Joseph Hallman	Alex Orr
Joseph F. Dery	Louis Purcil	Geo. O. Wilson	Frederick Davis
John W. Papel	Maurice Kelly	Wm. M. Mroseske	Frederick Taylor
Thomas L. Hogan	Oscar Reidel	Louis A. Stoecklin	Paul Mack
Julius J. Cummings	Jos. Lewandowski	Robert L. Cody	Carl Smith
Michael S. Donaghue	Frederick Stolp	Edward N. Milton	John Charles Ashby
Anthony Korte	Edward L. Vernier	Stanley Jankowski	Frank Roeback
Moses Fortune	Clarence W. Belleau	Jos. R. Schneider	Joseph Falkiewicz
Timothy Keohane	George McPhee	Harold A. Schaening	Leonard Grice
August W. Regentine	Louis Digut	Ernest Fox	Donald Barr
George S. Hough	James F. Thornton	Stanley Hausch	Stanley Lada
Michael L. Sheahan	Aubrey Chamberlin	Joseph M. Donnelly	Frank Vuichard
James A. Biggio	Andrew Nolan	Harry Schlotzhauer	Alwyn Girardot
Davis	Anthony J. Doemer	Oliver J. Strong	Robert Lee
James R. Dowdov	Frank Domagalski	Albert A. Austin	Thomas Killion
Louis A.	Malcolm O. Baxter	Charles B. Parish	Edward Dugelar
John	Patrick Black	Paul J. Reiner	Bruno Vanderski
James A. Connors	Thomas J. Sullivan	Raymond A. Benedict	Stanley Myatt
Charles J. Hale	Wendell P. Loderoot	Fred J. Bergman	Leo Yeanoplos
Cornelius Vecchio	Niel J. Christianson	John Gibbons	Joseph Makie
Richard Murphy	Walter Sweeney	Clay Carpenter	Ross J. Klemet
	Harvey Peterman	Charles Regnier	Terence M. McHugh
Michael J. Nevill	George Hawkins	Chauncey Wilmot	Edward G. Gargol
George M. Aylsworth	Edward E. Stephens	Elmer Morrell	Steve Mirka
Milton J. Emhoff	Edward B. Whalen	Joseph Bergin	Chester Pierce
Davis A. Brown	Robert J. Hammel	Charles Philips	William P. Ponton
Levi T. Fletcher	Alfred Huether	Clifford Barkoff	Earl Dunlap
Arthur A. Fitch	David Mitchel	James Daggett	Thaddeus Potocki
Louis J. Rosen	Joseph E. Jones	Harry Stahlnabel	James W. Blastow

The World Of A Firefighter . .

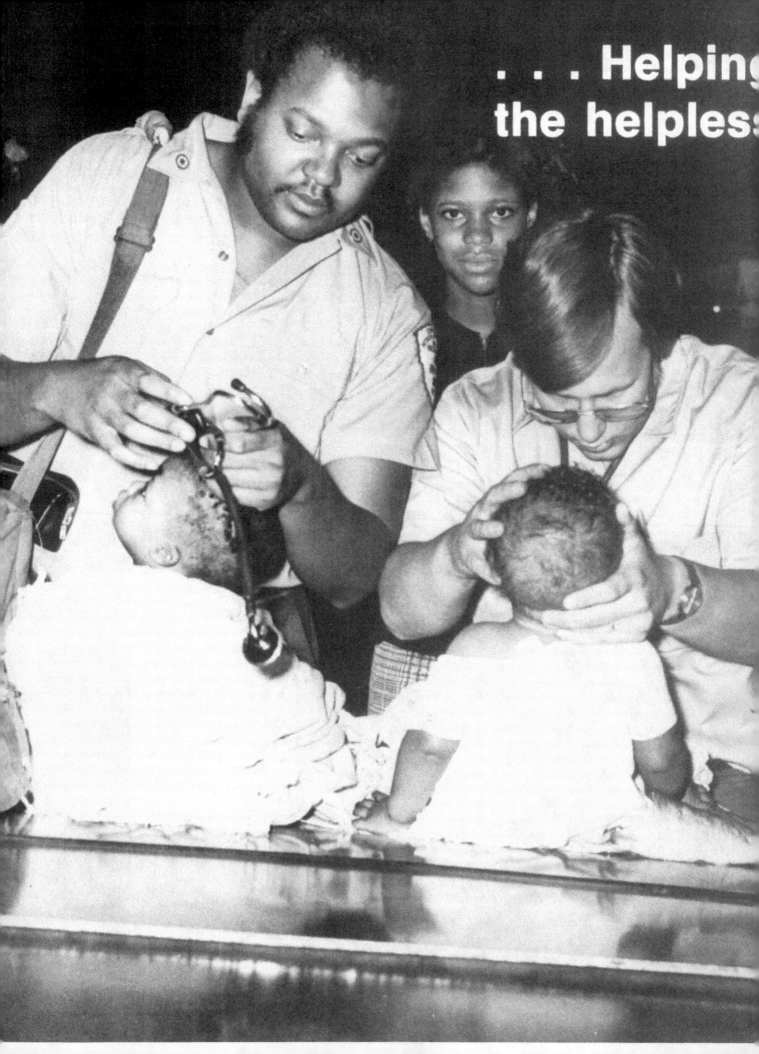

LEADERSHIP

The new City Charter adopted by the vote of the people of the City of Detroit effective July 1, 1974 mandated that the Fire Department have a paid Fire Commissioner in lieu of a 4-man, unpaid, Board of Fire Commissioners.

Under the new Charter, not only is the Fire Commissioner an appointed position, but also that of Deputy Fire Commissioner, Chief of Fire Department (in charge of Fire Fighting Operations) and the Fire Marshal.

DETROIT FIRE DEPARTMENT ORGANIZATION CHART

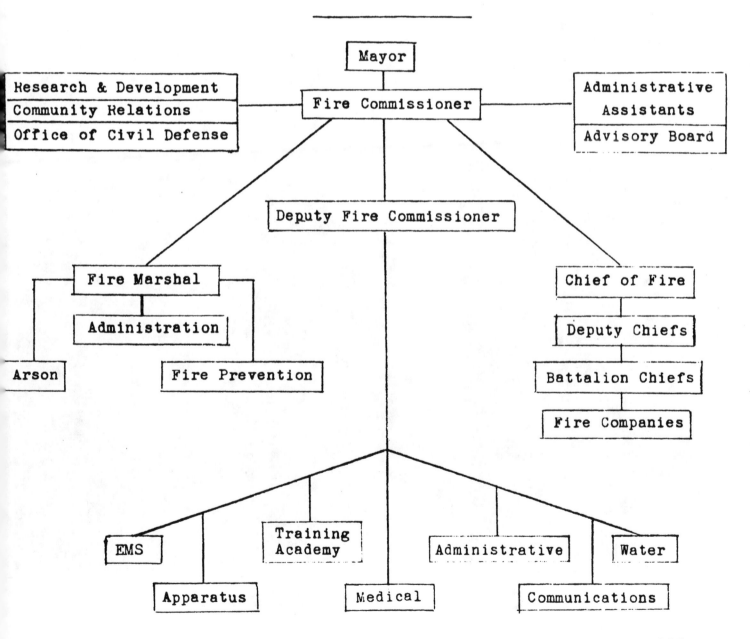

Commissioner Melvin Jefferson

Deputy Commissioner Phillip Gorak

Division Heads

THEODORE PHILLIPS
Chief of Fire Fighting
Operations

DONALD ROBINSON
Fire Marshall

DANIEL P. BOJALAD
Chief of E.M.S.

ROBERT KOSTER
Chief of Training

DR. J. R. DUNCAN, M.D.
Senior Fire
Examining Physician

MAURICE P. ROCHE
Chief Of
Communications

JOSEPH PAQUIN
Superintendent of
Apparatus

CHARLEY STEEL
Water Supply
Coordinator

LOUIS OLDANI
Administrative Clerk

JAMES T. ADAMS
Director of Civil
Defense

As we pieced together this historical century, we realize the backbone of the department is the FIREFIGHTER,—their insignia, their badges, the Cross of Malta. Thus the only suitable cover insignia is our department badge. Each man has a number, therefore, the selection of a specific number to represent all is paramount,—one which will represent all firefighters of our department with dignity and pride. After careful consideration we chose the number 600 (perhaps half of todays firefighting force in our very necessary service to the citizens of this city.) Our reason is much greater. It was the badge number of one of the most distinguished, gentle and dedicated men ever to avail himself to the fire service.

Joining the department February 18, 1917 as a sub at Engine Co. #32, he remained a member of that company until September 1917 at which time he became a member of the 32nd division in WW1 and returned to the department in February 1919. He progressed upward as each has and ended his very active career as Chief of Department on December 30, 1958,-a period of 41 years, 11 months service.

At this point, most just retire and find other avenues in which to spend their time and energies. In this case our member is still attending all Officer Club meetings, most retirement parties, visiting shut-ins and assisting retired members or their widows.

In October 1968, he initiated the Retirees Appreciation Fund. To this point he has collected over $56,000 for the benefit of Local 344 and its membership. Born in Luther, Michigan on March 7, 1897, now past 80 years of age, he is still very active in every phase of life. Across this great country, no department has a greater record nor has there been a more distinguished person to represent all of our firefighters.

We take extreme pleasure in dedicating this historical record to our Retired Chief of Department, RAY VALLAD.

Joseph Bolone
Captain

Captain
Jay W Smith

Sincerely,

Clarence C. Woodard
Historian

Detroit Fire Department
Board Of Fire Fighting Chiefs

FRONT ROW, (left to right) Seated — Edwin Ward, Frank Szopko, Michael Purcell, Deputy Chief Robert Case, Chief of Department Theodore Phillips, Deputy Chief Lawrence Rivard, Charles Cramer, Edward Tujaka, Martin Snarski. 2nd ROW — Ludwig Rupprecht, Frank Pospiech, Kenneth Gabriel, Stanley Zell, Andrew Rushford, Carl Byrum, Charles Fisher, John Gargulinski. 3rd ROW — Anthony Spezia, George DeCaussin, Walter Thursam, Walter Chapman, John Fusting, Edward Smith, Richard Avey.

Detroit Firefighters Association

EXECUTIVE BOARD (Left to right) — Raymond Zaborski, Treasurer — Andrew J. Dempsey, Secretary — Earl J. Berry, President — Hubert Gersch, Vice President

DIRECTORS, (SEATED, left to right) — George Nikoriuk, Joseph Bozich, Victor Nevin, Roger Lesniak, Leo Stevens. (STANDING) — Tim McConnell, Richard Robertson, Thomas McInchak, Michael Markowski, John Chakan, Joseph Portelli, Leonard Balcer.

Advisory Board Of Commissioners

FATHER BOGUS
not in picture

JOHN GAYLORD

VIRGIL SMITH

MARGARET JONES

Medical Division

DR. JAMES R. DUNCAN
Senior Fire Examining
Physician

DR. W. JONES MOSEE
Fire Examining Physician

DR. EDWARD C. LOCKHART
Fire Examining Physician

Detroit Firemen's Fund Association Board Of Trustees — 1977

SEATED, (left to right) — Clyde Jaynes, treasurer; Frederick Nicholls, president; George Leone, secretary; George Younan, vice-president.
STANDING — Leonard Zembrzuski, Donald Reusch, Neil Gurski, Iver Thornburg, Harold Christensen.

Since 1825 . . .

A Brief History Of Firefighting

Actually firefighting is as old as history itself. Since primitive man was driven from his early cave shelter by forest fires started by lightning, he has sought ways to control it.

The ancient Greeks and Egyptians were our first firefighters. In 440 B.C., the first fire extinguisher was the invention of a Greek writer and soldier named Appolodorus, who conceived the idea of a fire extinguisher fashioned from the bladder of an Ox and filled with water.

In 200 B.C., Heron, an Egyptian, invented the principle of the first piston type force pump which was used in all the early hand engines, and continued to be used in the steam and early automobile pumpers.

During the regime of Caesar Augustus in 6 A.D., the first public fire fighting companies were organized consisting of slaves, their equipment consisted of siphon pumps and buckets.

After the decline of the Greek and Roman civilization which was followed by centuries of general ignorance and superstition, known as the dark ages, fire engines were forgotten for possibly 1,300 years.

The Sixteenth Century was the era of the Re-discovery and development of the earlier fire engines and in the year 1518, crude fire engines were introduced in Germany.

It was a Dutchman in 1672, that invented the leather fire hose, and to England goes the honor of inventing the first practical hand engine in 1721. These early engines had to be filled with water provided by a bucket brigade.

In 1721, the first practical and successful hand operated fire engine was produced by Richard Newsham in London, England. The engine was a tub-type, goose-neck machine which had to be filled by buckets. The engine featured a piston pump and was the first type to use long wooden handle bars known as "brakes".

1732 was the year that the first American fire engine was built in Philadelphia by Anthony Nichols.

In 1737, the World's first organized fire engine company, manned by volunteers was also formed in Philadelphia by Benjamin Franklin.

Messrs. Sellers & Pennock, of Philadelphia introduced the first riveted leather fire hose. This new method of securing the seams in fire hose eliminated the troublesome hand-sewn leaky hose used since 1672.

To London, England goes the credit for inventing the steam fire engine. In 1829, John Ericsson & George Braithwaite built the World's first steam fire pumper.

To America goes the credit for perfecting the steam fire engine. In 1841, John Rapsey Hodge built the first practical steamer. The unit weighed 8 ton, was 13½ feet long and was operated by the Pearl Hose Co. No. 28 of New York City. This first American engine was declared impractical by the members of the volunteer company operating it for a period of two years. The steamer was removed from service and spent its remaining life operating at a paper box factory.

The chemical fire engine was developed in England using soda and acid. Chemical engines were introduced in America in 1860. By 1910, 90% of all our fires were extinguished by these machines. Booster water tanks were introduced in 1913, and by 1935 chemical tanks were replaced by the more practical and less costly booster tanks.

Hook and ladder trucks were introduced into the firefighting profession in 1790, and hose reels were invented in 1805.

It was not until 1822, that the suction engine was developed in America which forever eliminated the bucket brigades.

As the cities grew larger and the buildings became taller the hand engines were soon found to be ineffective. The first steam fire engine was invented in London, England and could pump 250 gallons of water per minute. Later, the steam fire engine was perfected in the United States and the first paid steam fire engine company went into service in Cincinnati, Ohio in 1852. This marked the era of horse drawn fire apparatus.

Self-propelled steamers were introduced in 1872, and it was in the year 1900 when the horses went under the hood and the first gasoline propelled fire pumper made its appearance. Fire department horses faded from the scene in most major cities in 1922.

Our Colonial Firefighters

A tribute to the small army of men who make up our great Fire Department—men who are dedicated to a career of saving life and property from man's worst enemy—Fire.

By Clarence C. Woodard
D.F.D. Historian

One of the most picturesque segments of Detroit's city life and cause for civic pride prior to the Civil War was the Volunteer Fire Department. These men, in their red shirts and white helmets, were among the gay blades of the town. They were young men of prospects or means. Being a fireman was so much fun one didn't always have time to attend fires, what with excursions, parades, dances, contests and other social obligations. The frequent fires which broke out would test the competition and skills between the companies, which, in turn, would be rewarded by grateful citizens with great quantities of refreshments.

Service in these early fire companies was voluntary and without monetary compensation. Membership was decided entirely by election. The firemen also elected their own foreman and other officers by ballot. Members lavished money on dress uniforms, silver trophies, and decorations for their engines.

Although the city bought the hand-operated pumping engines, the firemen bought nearly everything else, even in some cases, items for their fire halls. However, their responsibility to the citizens of Detroit was, for the most part, theoretical, and at times they sought political power. They had lots of color, but little efficiency, and almost no discipline. Today discipline and efficiency come before everything else in the Fire Department, and what was once a hobby has now become a profession and a science.

Detroit's first engine was imported from England by the British Military Command. It was a crude, hand-tub affair which had to be filled with buckets. The machine was built by Richard Newsham of London, and arrived on March 5, 1778. The engine cost 373.16 pounds (approximately $1,500 including transportation) and was placed in charge of a Thomas Williams. The population of Detroit was about 2,000 at the time.

After the Americans took over Detroit from the British, in 1796, they made the first effort to organize the citizens in case of fire on February 9, 1798. Article 9 of the early fire regulations said: ". . . on the first notice of fire assemble at the engine house to take the engine to the fire, and there to work as it may be judged the most expedient . . ."

Detroit was incorporated as a town and governed by a "Board of Trustees" in 1802, and one of the first acts of the "Board" was to establish a new fire ordinance posted in both English and French, so all citizens could read it. This new ordinance "Regulations for Securing the Town of Detroit from Injuries by Fires" required householders and shopkeepers to provide leather buckets, water-filled barrels, ladders of sufficient length to reach the highest level as well as "fire-bags" to carry goods from stores or homes in case of fire.

It was also required that chimneys be swept every two weeks between October and April, and every four weeks the rest of the year. Failure to do so was punishable by a five-dollar fine, the fine to be doubled in case a householder's chimney took fire. So that housewives' linen might not be soiled, the ordinance provided that the sweeping be done on Saturdays before 9:00 a.m. Two fire inspectors were appointed to enforce the new ordinance. In 1803, it was further ordered by the Council that all male citizens were to turn out at the cry of "Fire"! Failure to do so was punishable by a fine of two dollars or imprisonment for not more than two weeks.

On June 11, 1805, the entire village of Detroit consisting of two hundred wooden buildings burned to the ground, with the exception of one storehouse. The fire originated in a stable at the rear of Harvey's Bakery on the north side of Jefferson. As the flames spread, nearly all buildings were destroyed with a loss of $200,000. It is believed the first fire engine was used to little avail and was destroyed by the flames.

The second fire engine to be placed in operation was assembled in 1816, by local craftsmen, from an old bilge pump which had seen service on the Commodore Perry flagship during the War of 1812.

As the 1816 makeshift engine was frequently in need of repairs and of little value, a meeting was called at the "Council House" on April 9, 1821, to consider the purchase of a fire engine. As a result of the meeting, $400 was voted for the purchase. In 1823, the first engine house was constructed at Bates and East Larned Streets. It was provided with a large bell triangle to be used as a fire alarm. The following year, Peter Berthelet was granted authority to build a pump station at the foot of Randolph Street to supply the city with water. Early in 1825, the first Tamarack water mains were laid in Larned, Congress and Jefferson, and on September 25, 1825, the Common Council appointed and confirmed a fire department.

On December 26, 1825, the new fire engine, built by Jacob Smith of New York, arrived aboard the Schooner Superior. With this date, the great era of our Volunteer Fire Department began. The new engine was called "Protection No. 1," and was in service for 30 years. When a new engine was bought the old engine was given to the new company, and this old engine was therefore the first engine of six successive companies in turn. After the engine was retired, it was used in Fourth of July parades drawn about on a platform. The "Protection" Engine Company motto was: "Deeds are fruits, words are but leaves."

A second hand-engine company was organized on March 31, 1827, known as "Eagle" Engine Company No. 2. They used the original cantonment engine after it had been repaired, and their station house was erected on the northeast corner of Fort and Griswold Streets. In 1830, the company received a new engine costing $450.

"Wolverine" Engine Company No. 3 was formed, composed of the younger men of the community, as well as a new Hook and Ladder company early in 1830. On April 29, 1830, Engine Companies 1, 2, and 3, and the new "Rescue" Hook and Ladder Company took part in the first firemen's parade at the Public Wharf. The population of Detroit had grown to 2,222 at this time.

The city's first two 20,000 gallon reservoirs were constructed in 1832 on Jefferson at Bates and at Jefferson and Griswold. Along with the reservoirs, there were now fire mains along the principal streets equipped with hollowed tamarack log fire hydrants placed upright in the fire main. The flow of water from the hydrant was controlled with a wooden plug. They were protected from freezing in the winter months by enclosing them in boxes filled with manure.

On October 8, 1834, "Lafayette" Company No. 4 was

Detroit's first practical fire engine, "Protection No. 1". Built by Jacob Smith of New York and delivered on December 26, 1825. The engine served the City 30 years.

organized with a new hand engine along with 250 feet of riveted leather hose. Their motto was: "At danger's call we're prompt to fly, and bravely do or bravely die." In 1836, Common Council offered a reward of five dollars for the person first giving an alarm of fire by ringing the bell. The following year, the city took over the waterworks, and additional water mains were laid in 1838.

Still another fire engine company was formed in August, 1845 known as "Phoenix" Company No. 5, and a new station house was built at Clifford and Griswold Streets. The motto lettered on the back of their engine read: "Ready, Aye Ready. 'Man the brakes and keep me clean, and I'll take the butt from any machine.'"

One year later, in 1846, "Michigan" Company No. 6 was formed, and following a disastrous fire in downtown Detroit in 1848, "Union" Fire Company No. 7, and "Mechanics" No. 8 were formed in January, 1849.

With Detroit's population at 21,000 and shipping its greatest industry, our second ladder company was formed in 1850, called "Relief" Hook & Ladder Company No. 2, and their motto was: "We Raze to Save." Five years later, in 1856, "Detroit" Engine Company No. 9 was formed and their house was located on Gratiot near Beaubien. The next three-hand engine companies were formed in 1857, as "Operative" Engine Company No. 10, "Hamtramck" Spouters No. 11, and "Woodbridge" Engine Company No. 12. The "Woodbridge" Company was the last of the Volunteer Engine Companies to be formed.

At the sound of the alarm the volunteers would rush to the engine house and seize the ropes to the engine. Then, they would haul the engine through the streets to the fire. At the fire, a suction hose would be thrust into a cistern, connected to a hydrant or placed in the Detroit River; then the men would pump on the handles (brakes, as they were called). By pumping vigorously they raised a stream of water to fight the balze.

Service in the early engine companies were entirely voluntary, and membership eventually became a much-sought honor. In those days parades, demonstrations and contests were gala occasions. The firemen were clad in red shirts and black pantaloons, and the engines in parades were wreathed in flowers and decked with solid silver nameplates.

During tournaments, hand-engine companies that could "push" their engines to squirt the longest, highest and largest stream of water were declared the victors. These contests drew most of the citizens to watch, and the engine of the triumphant company was mounted with an immense broom, as it had swept the contest. To say, "She carries the broom" was to speak with highest praise.

In the Volunteer Fire Department, rivalry among the members eventually became so keen that many times their eagerness for competition endangered the lives and property of our citizens. Even at fires, one company would go so far to cut the leather hose of another in order to gain advantage over their rival! Such an occurrence gripped the attention of the town in 1854 when an old building caught fire at Larned and Wayne Streets (on the site where Fire Department Headquarters is presently located.) A fight broke out between the members of Engine Companies No. 2 and No. 8 to determine which company was to connect to the hydrant first. The building burned down and public indignation ran high after the event, but not as high as when the firemen went on strike because the Council refused to let them drag their heavy equipment over the wooden sidewalks of the city, which the firemen often did due to the poor condition of the streets. The Council's refusal was actuated by citizens who had complained with the hubs of the unwieldy engines too often ripped out pickets from the fences that surrounded nearly every home of this period, as well as endangered lives of pedestrians.

On April 24, 1855, the Council prohibited this practice between 6:00 a.m. and 10:00 p.m. This displeased a number of firemen and after a meeting on May 2, 1855, the members of Hand Engines 1, 4, 5, 6, 7, and 8 abandoned their engines and left the service. The firemen decided that such curtailment of their privileges demanded a demonstration. Heretofore, they had held not only the safety of the city in their care, but the balance of political power as well, and neither the Council nor the citizens dared ignore their requests. So,

The original fire engine house to be located on Clifford St. at Griswold. Erected in 1845 by "Phoenix" No. 5 a hand engine company, they later changed their name to "Washington" Co. No. 5. This building was razed in 1858 and replaced by a newer two story engine house at a cost of $4,590. In 1856, John Hopkins immortalized this Phoenix fire house in oils and the painting still hangs in headquarters.

they paraded through the streets with helmets reversed in protest, and after consuming a great deal of beer and whiskey in their hall at Jefferson and Randolph Street, they threatened to thrash the members of the Council one by one. They declared, until the Council reversed its ruling, they would fight no more fires.

But for once, the firemen in their arrogance had misjudged the public's patience. Within two days, on June 13, 1855, Common Council manned each engine company with a fresh crew consisting of prominent citizens, and former members who had tendered their services. The new companies were more mannerly than the old, and more efficient. On their rosters were such famous names as Zachariah Chandler, James A. Van Dyke, John Owen, Chauncey Hurlbut, George L. Whitney and many others. No longer could disreputable persons join the Volunteer Fire Companies to gain political power!

The old companies had left the city unprotected for days at a time while they went on jaunts to other cities. The new ones installed watchmen in the tower of the old-old City Hall, which stood Cn Cadillac Square, atop the old Russell House and in the steeples of the State Street and Jefferson Avenue Churches. And the firemen stayed on the job.

Detroit's first central fire alarm, a steel triangle that, when struck could drown out any bell in the city, was hung in the old-old City Hall cupola in March, 1857. A year later in September, a Silsby steam pumper on its way to delivery in Chicago, was tested on Campus Martius, competing for three days with the hand-operated engines No. 8 and 10.

The horse-drawn steamer, although slower to start, proved steadier and more powerful than the hand pumpers. The Council ordered one built for $3,150 by the Amoskeag Manufacturing Company of Manchester, New Hampshire. It was delivered in October, 1860, and was manned by Detroit's first paid firemen. Thus, the age of mechanization — and fire fighting by professionals — had come to Detroit.

On June 14, 1861, the last parade of the "Old Volunteer Fire Department" in uniform was held. The units consisted of seven hand and two steam fire engine companies. As the volunteer companies were beginnig to disband, on July 21, 1861, Common Council provided for a paid hand engine, and hook and ladder company to augment the new steamers. Shortly afterwards, four additional hand companies were

established consisting of 23 men each. The foreman received $200 a year, firemen $100 a year, and the hook and ladder men received $120 a year. Finally, in the month of February, 1865, with the arrival of the fourth steam fire engine, Common Council formally disbanded all hand-engine companies.

Reminders of these early volunteers such as: helmets, trumpets, red shirts, uniform belts, buckets, and an early hand pumper and hose reel are on display at the Detroit Historical Museum located on Woodward Ave. at Kirby.

When the Volunteer hand companies were being replaced by paid steam companies, many citizens complained that progress was destroying one of the fine American institutions. There were similar complaints when the gasoline propelled fire apparatus threatened to replace the picturesque horse-drawn steamers. In 1867, by an act of the State Legislature (so it would be removed fr om local politics) a four-man Fire Commission was organized. The establishment of this Commission, with a fully professional group of firefighters was observed in the month of October, 1967 with a huge Centennial Parade of fire apparatus from both the Detroit area and Canada.

The steam fire engine era in Detroit between 1860 and 1922 was noted for the thrilling spectacle of galloping horses pulling a shining, smoking steamer through the streets. In 1874, the Detroit department received its first piece of self-propelled equipment — a huge Amoskeag steam engine that could travel through the streets at 15 miles per hour under its own steam power. Because of its lack of speed it did not prove popular, and was the only one purchased.

Not long after the turn of the century, when the efficiency of the internal combustion engine could no longer be denied, the department organized its first automobile company in October, 1908, with a Packard "Flying Squadron" unit known as Engine Co. No. 30.. The Detroit Historical Museum has one of these Packard squad cars in its collection. The first motorized pumping engine was placed in service in 1910, and by April, 1922, the gasoline propelled fire apparatus had completely displaced the horse. Another fire-fighting weapon, radio dispatching, was introduced in 1929 when a transmitter was installed in the Fire Alarm Office and a receiver in the fire-boat "John Kendall". The original call-letters were WKDT and in January, 1949 when the first two-way sets were installed the original call-letters were changed to KQA 205.

Today, the Detroit Fire Department Firefighting Division consists of 42 Engine, 28 Ladder companies, 9 Tactical Mobile Squads, a hose company, an engine at the Detroit City Airport, a department ambulance and a future fire boat now on the drawing board. The Fire Department maintains its own Training Academy and other divisions such as: Administration, Apparatus, Communications, Civil Defense, Emergency Medical Service, Fire Marshal, Medical and Water Supply.

Detroit's seal and motto are based on the fire which wiped out the frontier village in 1805 and was adopted by the City Council on May 10, 1829. "Speramus Meliora" (We hope for better things) — "Resurget Cinerbus" (It shall rise again from the ashes), still remains a defiant challenge to civic misfortune.

In this modern era when a fire engine thunders past with screaming siren, it is a reminder of the long way firefighting has come from the bucket brigade and hand engine volunteers. Through intensive and continuous training, the high standards and efficiency of our Detroit Fire Department have placed it among the great departments in the United States and in the world.

"Detroit" Fire Company No. 9 - Organized June 10, 1856. The entire crew of fifty men turned out for this 1857 photo shortly after the company received their new manual engine. The hand pumper was built by James Smith of New York, featured a short stroke piston pump and was 24 feet in length. Their station house was located on the north side of Gratiot between Beaubien & St. Antoine. John Kendall was Foreman of the company.

"Neptune Engine Co. No. 6". Originally organized in 1846, the company was called Michigan Engine Co. No. 6 and nicknamed "Rough and Ready". In 1855 the name was changed to Neptune Engine Co. No. 6. This company provided their own fire engine, hose and all other expenses from their own funds for the first year of operation. The company proudly display their new Button & Blake hand engine. Their engine house was located at E. Larned & St. Antoine.

Detroits
Fire
Horses

When Pavements Rang To Galloping Hoofs—Detroit's Fire Horses

By Clarence Woodard and Walter McCall

Similar scenes had already been enacted in many American cities. Detroit's turn came on the afternoon of April 10, 1922. The most colorful era in the Detroit Fire Department's 97-year history was about to come to a close.

More than 50,000 Detroiters lined Woodward Ave. from Grand Circus Park to Cadillac Square, to watch the last five horses in the department make their final run. Adding irony to the sad occasion was the fact that there would be no "fire" at that last alarm.

On signal, Pete, Jim and Tom dashed from their stalls in Engine 37's quarters at Central and Dix and took their places at the front of the big steamer. Babe and Rusty took theirs in front of the hose wagon. Nostrils flaring and hoofs flashing, the gallant steeds galloped out of the firehouse and into history.

At the end of the run, downtown, the fire department band was there to play Auld Lang Syne. Grizzled veterans of the department, who had loved and lived with the horses, were there, too. There were more than a few moist eyes in the crowd that day.

Even before the commemorative run was over, shiny, new motor trucks had taken the places of the horses in Engine 37's quarters. Progress, yes. But something was lost. It is hard to believe that half a century has passed since that memorable day.

Some 500 horses served the Detroit Fire Department from the advent of the steam fire engines until the next major technological change arrived with the internal combustion gasoline auto in the early years of this century. No man who lived in that era failed to thrill to the thundering hoofbeats, flying sparks and sheer spectacle of magnificently-trained teams drawing the smoke-belching steamer over cobblestone pavements.

Detroit's early fire protection needs were well served by volunteer fire companies that manned hand-drawn, hand-operated firefighting equipment. But by October, 1860, professional paid firemen and the first steam fire engine sealed the fate of the hand-operated engines. For the next half century, horses pulled the puffing steamers, the hose wagons and the lumbering hook and ladder trucks.

Even the chiefs rode to fires behind beautifully-groomed animals, and horses provided the motive power for the Water Tower and fuel wagons.

The firemen became very proud and fond of their superb horses. These fine animals seemed to be born and bred for the fire service— just as many men joined the department for the challenge and romance the job offered. The love of a man for his horses was as stirring and noble as any love could be, and many of these fine animals sacrificed their lives so that the

Detroit's first horse drawn hose reel carriage. The unit was organized along with our first steam fire engine company in October, 1960. By 1893, the department had replaced all similar hose carriages with hose wagons.

Volunteer "Minute Men" and regular paid members of "Phoenix Steam Fire Engine Co. No. 3". The company was the third steam fire engine company to be formed in Detroit and was organized on July 24, 1861. The station house located on Clifford St. at the head of Griswold was erected in 1858 to serve a hand engine company. This photo was taken on April 25, 1865, as the company was preparing to participate in President Lincoln's Funeral Parade in our city. This same company, along with Engine 6, was sent to the city of Chicago by special train to assist their firemen in the great fire of October, 1871.

lives of men might be saved.

Grown men and legion numbers of small boys never outgrew the thrill of being around the firehouse when the bells hit. One had to have quick eyes to catch the action the following few seconds would bring.

When the alarm sounded, the firemen on watch would release a spring lock on the horse stalls. The doors would fly open, the horses would jump to their feet and gallop to the harness suspended overhead in front of the engine. As soon as the collars were clicked, they were off out the door and on their way to the fire. Because they knew they were being watched, the fire horses pranced out of the house as proud as show horses.

Although bells would sound in the station many times through the day, the fire horses seemed to instinctively know the ones that called them out.

When leaving the station and seeing a serious fire up ahead, the driver would sometimes stand up on the footboard, whip in one hand and reins in the other, urging his animals on as fast as they could go. The rumbling engine would sway from side to side and the stoker hanging on at the rear would grip the handrails for his life.

The firemen became close friends with their horses, teaching them tricks and enjoying the mutual affection. At big fires, the horses were unharnessed from their engines and led away to a cooler, safer place. In winter months they were covered with blankets.

The character of the service performed by the fire horses was essentially different from that required of horses in any other line. An ideal fire horse had to

Stalwart members of the "Rescue Hook & Ladder Co. No. 1", proudly pose in front of their new 1870, rear-steer ladder truck. The photo was taken in front of the new addition to the old remodeled Washington Market Building at W. Larned & Wayne Streets. This horse drawn ladder truck was the first one to be purchased by the new paid fire department and was built by the C. E. Hartshorn Co. of New York at a cost of $2,500. The name "Rescue" was dropped from the official name of the company along with other ladder company names in 1888.

possess exceptional intelligence, an even, strong temperament, tractability and perfection of body, limb and wind. The average purchase price was $240, and no horse was considered unless it was up to the required weight.

Horse weight required for hose wagon teams was 1,100 pounds each, and for engine and ladder truck teams 1,700 pounds each. Experience proved that it was not only sound economy to provide the finest equine specimens for fire department service, but it was extremely injudicious, both as to expense and good service, to put horses into active fire service without special training.

All Detroit Fire Department horses when purchases were given a numbered tag which was fastened to the halter. This tag would go with the horse from place to place. The average fire horse had a service life of about nine years and upon retirement was sold to a kindly farmer for the remainder of its days. Many of the department horses acquired nicknames like "Old Stub", "Little Joe", "Flora", or "Maggie", etc.

All Detroit steam pumpers were drawn by two-horse teams until 1893, when larger horses became more difficult and expensive to buy. As a result, the department converted all of its ladder trucks and steamers to three-horse draft. Hose wagons, replacing hose real carriages, were introduced the same year. Each steamer was accompanied by one of these hose wagons, drawn by two horses, and equipped with a 50-gallon soda and acid chemical tank, 300 feet of rubber chemical hose mounted on a reel, and carrying 1,000 feet of 2½-inch fire hose.

The most graceful running horses were generally used as center horses in a three-horse hitch. After each run the horses' shoes were examined to ensure that they were tight. The horses would lift their hoofs as the firemen made these rounds—they seemed to know the walk of their drivers when they entered the station and would look for them. When feeding time was near the horses would paw the floor of their stalls. If an alarm sounded while they were eating, the horses would stop and instinctively gallop to their harnesses.

In 1885 there were 76 horses in department service. Only the finest quality feed was bought, directly from the producer. The average cost of hay purchased that year was $11.58 per ton, and oats 28 cents a bushel. Actual cost of feeding a horse for the year was $57.07, or a fraction over 15½ cents a day.

The early training and supply stables in Detroit were at Russell and Calhoun (Erskine) Streets and consisted of several brick buildings at the rear of the "new" quarters of Hook and Ladder Co. No. 5. The stables had 35 open and box stalls for training and breaking in new horses. The facility also had a cinder track 14 feet wide around the lot that formed a 700-foot training course. Here, all new fire horses were trained under actual engine house conditions.

On May 1, 1885 the Fire Department Horse Bureau was established, with Allen Armstrong as Superintendent. By 1893, the D.F.D. had 180 horses under the supervision of Battalion Chief William J. Gowan, who assigned the animals to various fire companies, changing them around as circumstances required. A horse may have worked well in one house and refused duty in another—a complaint never heard of their motorized successors! It sometimes became necessary to take a horse out of quarters that were not congenial to a home that suited his tastes.

The entire crew, plus the mascot of "L. H. Cobb Steam Fire Engine Co. No. 7" pose for this photograph. The station house was erected in 1873, at the corner of E. Fort & Elmwood and the company went into service on February 1, 1874. When Engine 19 was placed in service in 1894, on E. Congress St. near Jos Campau, Engine 7 moved to the station house of Ladder 6, on Concord Ave., North of E. Jefferson and Ladder 6 moved to the Elmwood & Fort location. In 1923, the Elmwood Ave. station was rebuilt and Engine 19 moved in with Ladder 6. Engine Co. 19 was disbanded in 1949 as an economy move and Engine 7 moved back to the Elmwood station in 1950 with Ladder 6. The second station was razed in October, 1970 when both companies moved into the new modern station at E. Lafayette & Mt. Elliott Ave. Engine 7, was originally organized with both "Minute Men" and regular paid full time members and shown in the photo from left to right are: Richard (Dick) Jarrait, hose cart driver; Snyder, the mascot: Morris Cousino, pipeman; Don McClelland, engine driver; George Ring, pipeman; Jos. McKernen, Engineer & Foreman (hand on valve wheel); Louis Werner, pipeman (standing on engine platform); Jack Gordon; Jack Chandler and John Black, pipeman.

In the event that no alarms were received in any station in a period of 24 hours, the horses were hitched to a special wagon for 90 minutes each day and exercised in a three-block area around their station. Their regular harness was used, and should an alarm be received during the exercise period, they could be quickly called back to the station by the ringing of the station's tower bell, transferred to their regular apparatus and respond to the fire call.

The year 1910 was the peak for the number of horses in Detroit Fire Department service. Detroit had more than 250 horses which provided the motive power for 29 steam fire engines, 13 ladder trucks, 3 hose companies, the water tower and a number of Chiefs' and supply buggies.

But change was in the wind. Three years earlier, in 1907, a four-cylinder Oldsmobile was purchased for the Chief of Department and a Cartercar for the Superintendent of Apparatus. A Packard squad truck went into service in 1908, and in June, 1910 the first gasoline motor pumping engine went into service at Engine 3. The last horse-drawn steamer was bought in January, 1909.

In 1920 the horse population of Detroit was 35,000. In a spot near the Eastern Market, 500 horses were auctioned off almost every Saturday. Today, only the fine animals of the Detroit Police Department remain in the city.

Detroit's last remaining link with this romantic era are three steam fire engines. The 1904 LaFrance of "Steam Fire Engine Co. No. 6" is on display at the Detroit Historical Museum and another huge 1906 Amoskeag steamer can be seen at the Henry Ford Museum in Dearborn which was retired from Engine 1. Recently an old Ahrens engine has been painstakingly restored in the fire department's repair shop by members of the Box 42 Associates, a local organization of dedicated fire buffs. This Ahrens engine was formerly assigned to Engine 13 at Russell & E. Ferry and has been turned over to the Detroit Historical Museum to be used in local parades.

Steam Fire Engines In The Detroit Fire Department

D.F.D. Dept. No.	Mfg. No.	In Service Year	Month	Make	Pump Capacity G.P.M.		Class or Size of Engine	Cost	Engine Co.
None	22	1860	Oct.	Amoskeag	600		First	$3,150	1
''	26	1861	Jan.	'' ''	''		'' ''		2,8
''	30	1861	July	'' ''	''		'' ''	$3,250	1,3
''	101	1865	Feb.	'' ''	400		Second	$3,100	4,7
''	128	1865	June	'' ''	''		'' '' ''	'' '' ''	5
''	261	1868	April	'' ''	500		'' '' ''	$3,300	6
''	401	1871	Sept.	'' ''	600		First	$4,400	1,2
1	408	1872	Sept.	'' ''	500		Second	$4,250	5,29
None	430	1872	Sept.	'' ''	''		'' ''		10,22
''	447	1874	Jan.	'' ''	600		First	$4,620	1,3,9,10

(The above engine was self-propelled and converted to horse draft in 1890)

D.F.D. Dept. No.	Mfg. No.	In Service Year	Month	Make	Pump Capacity G.P.M.		Class or Size of Engine	Cost	Engine Co.
None	508	1876	May	'' ''	500		Second	$3,450	4
''	524	1877	Sept.	'' ''	''		'' '' ''	$3,540	7,18
''	Unknown	1880	Feb.	'' ''	600		First	$3,600	9,10
''	'' ''	1882	May	'' ''	''		''	$3,670	8,5,26
''	'' ''	1883	Sept.	Silsby	700		Second	- -	11
''	'' ''	1886	June	'' ''	800		First	$4,090	6
''	'' ''	1886	Dec.	'' ''	500		Fourth	- -	12
''	'' ''	1887	Jan.	'' ''	''		'' ''	- -	13,20
''	'' ''	1887	Aug.	'' ''	''		'' ''	- -	5,17
2 - -	518	1887	Oct.	Ahrens	800		First	$7,350	1,8,9,21
None	Unknown	1888	Feb.	Silsby	500		Fourth	- -	14
''	'' ''	1888	Dec.	Ahrens	''		Third	- -	15,22
3 - -	900	1889	Nov.	Clapp & Jones	''		Fourth	- -	27,33
4 - -	623	1890	Aug.	Ahrens	800		First	$7,620	6,7,15
6 - -	673	1891	Oct.	Amoskeag	900		'' ''	$8,130	3,19,14
7 - -	686	1893	Jan.	'' ''	1,100	Ext.	First	$8,800	1,13
8 - -	687	1893	Jan.	'' ''	'' ''	''	'' ''	'' ''	3,18
9 - -	701	1893	Dec.	'' ''	'' ''	''	'' ''	'' ''	2,7
12 - -	113	1896	May	Manning	1,000		First	- -	13,28,41
10 - -	347	1896	July	LaFrance	800		Second	- -	4,21,37
11 - -	2362	1896	July	American	''		'' ''	- -	14,12,38
13 - -	118	1897	Oct.	Manning	1,100		First	- -	8,17
None	Unknown	1898	Sept.	'' ''	600		Second	- -	15,23
''	'' ''	1899	Jan.	'' ''	''		'' ''	- -	11,20,28
14 - -	124	1899	Oct.	'' ''	500		Third	- -	21,24,22
5 - -	123	1899	Nov.	'' ''	1,100	Ext.	First	- -	1,3
15 - -	126	1900	Nov.	'' ''	'' ''	''	'' ''	- -	10,19
17 - -	127	1901	Nov.	'' ''	'' ''	''	'' ''	- -	11
18 - -	471	1901	Dec.	LaFrance	600		Second	- -	3,24,33
20 - -	490	1903	Sept.	'' ''	900		First	- -	19,28
21 - -	502	1904	Sept.	'' ''	''		'' ''	- -	8
22 - -	503	1904	Nov.	LaFrance	900		First	$7,600	6, Ext.

(The above engine, Dept. No. 22, is on exhibit at Detroit Hist. Museum)

D.F.D. Dept. No.	Mfg. No.	In Service Year	Month	Make	Pump Capacity G.P.M.		Class or Size of Engine	Cost	Engine Co.
23 - -	504	1904	Nov.	LaFrance	900		First	$7,600	5,17
24 - -	505	1904	Dec.	'' ''	''		'' ''	'' ''	3,12,14
25 - -	506	1905	Nov.	'' ''	''		'' ''	$7,890	9
26 - -	517	1905	Nov.	'' ''	''		'' ''	'' ''	2,20
27 - -	518	1905	Nov.	'' ''	''		'' ''	'' ''	4
29 - -	804	1906	June	Amoskeag	''		'' ''	- -	21
30 - -	805	1906	June	'' ''	''		'' ''	- -	15
28 - -	809	1906	June	'' ''	1,100	Ext.	First	- -	1,2

(The above engine is on exhibit at the Henry Ford Museum, Dearborn, Mich.)

D.F.D. Dept. No.	Mfg. No.	In Service Year	Month	Make	Pump Capacity G.P.M.		Class or Size of Engine	Cost	Engine Co.
31 - -	155	1908	Oct.	Ahrens	700		Second	- -	13,29

(The above engine was restored in 1973 through the combined efforts of Fine Trucks, Inc. of Mt. Clemens and the Box 42 Associates of Detroit)

D.F.D. Dept. No.	Mfg. No.	In Service Year	Month	Make	Pump Capacity G.P.M.		Class or Size of Engine	Cost	Engine Co.
32 - -	3234	1908	Dec.	LaFrance "Metropolitan"	700		Second	- -	23,37
33 - -	3235	1908	Dec.	'' ''	''		'' ''	- -	31
34 - -	3236	1908	Dec.	'' ''	''		'' ''	- -	26,32
36 - -	3233	1909	Jan.	'' ''	900		First	- -	20,38

The last steamer went out of service on April 7, 1922 at Engine Co. 37 and the last parade of the fire horses in dowtown Detroit was April 10th.

C. C. Woodard D. F. D. Historian

AMOSKEAG
Self Propelled Steam Fire Engine In The D.F.D.

This unusual contrivance was the one and only self-propelled steam fire engine in the Detroit Fire Department. The machine was an Amoskeag, built in Manchester, New Hampshire, by a division of the Manchester Locomotive Works. The unit was placed in service on January 12, 1874 at Engine Company No. 1, at Wayne and W. Larned Streets and was called the "Hercules".

The ackward but valiant engine astonished spectators as it went along the cobble stone streets under its own power. It weighed 5 tons, had a top speed of 15 miles per hour, cost $5,000 and antedated Henry Ford and Charles Brady King by at least a decade.

This was the very first power vehicle ever built with differential gears. The first self-propellers delivered to Boston and New York were not satisfactory because of the difficulty of negotiating corners while both rear wheels were turning at the same speed. This problem was solved with the Detroit machine.

Motive power was supplied by sprocket chains connecting a shaft on the pump and the rear wheels. The engineer controlled the speed of the apparatus from his position on the ash pan at the rear of the steamer, and the drivers duties were confined to steering and stopping the machine.

By February 15, 1875, the Fire Commission questioned its practicability. Naturally, its efficiency as a self propelled vehicle depended upon generating a good head of steam in a very short time. To accomplish this, forced draft was resorted to, and it was claimed that when responding to alarms of fire, sparks and embers blown from its stack frequently ignited roofs and awnings along the route. The return trip to the engine house was usually interrupted by numerous stops to extinguish these incipient fires. At any rate, the self-propeller had the reputation of starting more fires than it extinguished.

Ten years after being placed in service the machine was moved to Engine Company No. 3, in 1884. At the time, Engine 3 was located on Clifford Street at the head of Griswold Street. Due to the confusion in operating the machine as well as the poor performance at the D. M. Ferry Seed Co. fire on January 1, 1886, it was retired from active service as a self-propeller and no similar machines were ordered. The unit was converted to horse draft in 1890, and continued in active service for another 11 years at Engine 10.

C. Woodard

Historic Photos Of The Steam Engine Era

A "Minute Man" of 1876. A title supplementing regular firemen. They slept at the fire station, received $20 per month, worked at any job they chose by day - but day or night they responded to the fire alarm. This photo is of Pipeman Adolph Hoenighausen of "Phoenix" Steam Fire Engine Co. No. 3, then located on Clifford Street at the head of Griswold. Hoenighausen advanced in the ranks and retired as Captain of Engine Co. 23.

First Chemical Engine in the Detroit Fire Department. "Chemical Co. No. 1" went into service on October 1, 1876, at the original Headquarters Bldg. at Wayne & W. Larned Streets. The engine shown was built by The Babcock Chemical Engine Co. and consisted of two 80 gallon soda & acid chemical tanks connected to a hose reel with 200 feet of rubber hose. The unit weighed 5,160 lbs. when ready for service, cost $2,226 and was drawn by two horses. In the year 1899, on September the 8th the company became "Hose Co. 1".

On display on W. Larned Street, in front of the original fire headquarters building is the 1883, Hayes-LaFrance, horse drawn turntable aerial ladder truck of "Rescue Hook & Ladder Co. No. 1". Note, the tiller man's seat over the rear wheels and under the main ladder. The aerial ladder raised by a nut and screw device operated by a hand crank, could be extended to a height of 86 feet. The older two story building in the background was the original Washington Market Building erected in 1836, converted to a school in 1842, back to a market place in 1852 and remodeled in 1856 to a fire station for a hand engine and a hook & ladder company. The original building served as quarters for our first paid steam fire engine company in 1860 and the addition in the foreground was erected in 1870. The building was razed in 1888 and our second fire headquarters erected on the site in 1889.

Exercise buggy used in the Detroit Fire Department at the turn of the century. In the event the horses of any of our fire companies had no alarm response during a 24 hour period, these wagons were used to exercise the steeds by traveling the streets in the vicinity of the fire station. If an alarm was received while the horses were being exercised the house bell would be rung calling them back to the station.

This steam pumper was one of the highest developments of fire engines at the turn of the century. Built by Amoskeag, a division of the Manchester Locomotive Works of Manchester, N.H., the huge 1,100 gallon per minute went into service at Engine 1, in 1906. This engine was the largest such unit to be purchased by the city during the horse drawn era and was equipped with roller bearings and is now on permenant exhibit at the Henry Ford Museum in Dearborn, Michigan. The photo was taken in 1911 on Wayne St. Nr. Larned.

Taken in 1910, the huge Manning 1200 gpm. steamer of Engine 3 is shown responding to an alarm from the old station located on Clifford at the head of Griswold.

Shown in the photo is retired Fire Dept. Lt. Edward Cook. Taken in March, 1967 during a visit to Fire Headquarters, Mr. Cook was 77 years old at the time. Cook was the driver of the steam fire engine shown in the background which was a huge Amoskeag assigned to Engine Co. No. 1. Mr. Cook retired in 1936 and is shown holding a model steam fire engine built by Clarence Woodard.

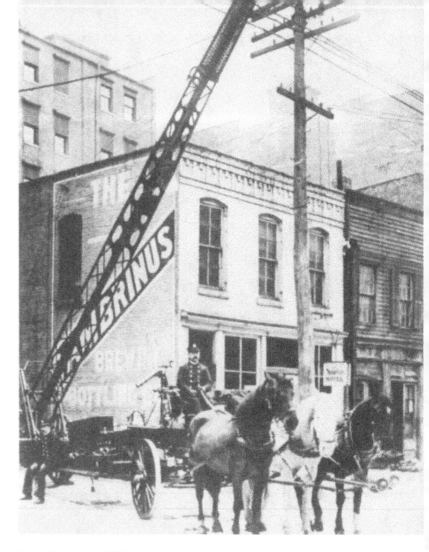

Detroit's original 1893 water tower taken shortly after the machine was sold to the Toledo, Ohio Fire Dept. in 1916.

Detroit's original water tower. The unit was built by the Fire Extinguisher Mfg. Co. of Chicago in 1893 and had a three horse hitch. The main tower was raised by a hand crank and screw device and mounted on a turntable. The telescopic, or second section, was drawn up to its required height by means of a crank and cable and could be raised to a height of 75 feet. Shown in the photo is the tower shortly after being purchased by the Toledo, Ohio Fire Department in 1916. Toledo installed the Christie gasoline powered front-drive unit a short time later and continued using the tower until 1961.

The last horse drawn ladder truck to be purchased by the Detroit Fire Department. Built by Seagrave, the unit was placed in service on January 11, 1911 at Ladder 15, then located on the east side of Woodward Ave. near Westminister. The truck featured a 65′ aerial ladder which was raised by a spring hoist mounted on a turntable. The truck was placed on a Ahrens-Fox gasoline propelled tractor in 1913.

It Came To A Glorious End

The famous last run of the fire horses in a parade along Woodward Ave. in downtown Detroit on April 10, 1922. Fifty thousand citizens lined the parade route to say farewell to the gallant horses which had served the department since 1860. Shown in the photograph was the LaFrance steamer of Engine Co. No. 37, the last fire company to use horsepower. Firemen were very fond of the stouthearted horses and gave them names. The three steeds pulling the steamer were Pete, Jim and Tom.

Then Came The Motor

A rare photo of Detroit's first motorized fire engines taken in front of the old station house of Engine 3, then located on Clifford Street at the head of Griswold. Both units were decorated with flags prior to a Fourth of July parade and were built by the Webb Fire Apparatus Co. in 1910. The company on the left, was Hose 1, with their combination hose and chemical truck and Michael Dwyer was the driver. The unit on the right, was the 700 gpm. pumper of Engine 3 and the man in the drivers seat was Elmer Murdock. Murdock was the first man in the department to learn about, and drive the new pumper. He was chosen for the task because he was the only one who owned an automobile and eventually instructed most of the other engine drivers as motorized equipment gradually replaced the horses. Standing on the running board at the extreme right of the photo is Walter F. Isreal, who became Chief of the Dept. on November 1, 1932.

It was in July, 1906 when the city of Detroit purchased 3 Carter Cars for the Fire Department Chiefs and they were the first gasoline propelled vehicles in the department. Shown in this photo is Chief James C. Broderick behind the wheel of his 1911 Oldsmobile. This four-cylinder Autocraft Model roadster was one of two delivered the same year.

The first Ahrens-Fox piston pumper in the Detroit Fire Department. Was placed in service on April 23, 1912 at Engine 18, Mt. Elliott near Sylvester and served that company until 1928. This was the second gasoline propelled pumper built by the famous Ahrens-Fox Co.

The first gasoline propelled tractor in the Detroit Fire Dept. Built by the Seagrave Corp. of Columbus, Ohio, this six cylinder, air-cooled model went in service at Ladder 1. The unit was placed under the 85' aerial truck that was purchased in 1908 from Seagrave and was originally horse drawn. This 1912 tractor was nicknamed "The Bull Moose".

Dashboard gadgets were no problem on this rig. The crew of Ladder Co. No. 6, proudly show off their new Christy gasoline propelled front-drive tractor in 1916. This 85 foot aerial truck was delivered in 1908, was the first spring hoist aerial truck in the department as well as the first LaFrance unit to be purchased by the city. Originally horse drawn, the tractor was added eight years later.

Seagrave 350 gpm. pumping engine and chemical car. Delivered to the Detroit Fire Dept. in 1917, the unit was quartered with Engine 3 and was listed on the running cards as Engine 3-A. The unit was nicknamed "Booster 3", ran with Engine 3 and was the only engine company in the department to carry two chemical tanks, a life net and deck turret nozzle.

DETROIT FIRE DEPARTMENT
PACKARD HOSE WAGON

This 1921 Packard combination chemical and hose car was one of seven similar units which saw service in the department from 1921 to 1938. They were powered by a 26 horsepower engine, had a deck monitor nozzle, two 40 gallon soda & acid chemical tanks and a reel containing 300 feet of 1-inch rubber chemical hose. The unit carried the following equipment: 800 feet of 2½-inch hose, 100 feet of 3-inch hose, two axes, 2 play-pipes, one pike pole, one 20-foot extension and one 12-foot roof ladder, plus one hose roller. The Packard shown was Dept. No. 364, and ran with the Seagrave pumper of Engine 11. Other identical units served Engine Companies; 4, 7, 8, 28, 29, & 32 at the time. All of these hose wagons along with two Packard service ladder truck tractors were all retired from active service in 1938.

Interior of Detroit's High Pressure Pumping Station at the foot of Randolph St. The building was erected in 1921 at a cost of $145,057, plus an additional $167,325 for constructing the wharf. The High Pressure system went in service in 1922 along with the related hydrant system being completed in the downtown high value area and along the waterfront. Shown, are the 6 Dean Hill Multi-Stage Pumps used to supply the system. Each powered by 700 H.P. motors and could deliver 2,500 GPM. at 300# pressure. Due to restrictions by the Health Dept., Civic Center, Freeway and Urban Renewal construction, the High Pressure System was placed out of service in the month of March, 1956.

The 1916 Seagrave hose and chemical car of Hose Co. No. 1. The photo was taken on April 10, 1922, during the parade commemorating the last run of the fire horses. The apparatus was Factory Serial No. 15105, Dept. No. 274 and went in service in May, 1916 at fire headquarters. The unit was rebuilt in 1922 by Seagrave with two 2,000 gpm. turret deck guns and became High Pressure Co. 3 in the quarters of Engine 8. The truck was sold for scrap in 1956 when the High Pressure System was discontinued.

Detroit's famous Seagrave water tower. A familiar sight at downtown alarms for more than a quarter century was the huge apparatus helped subdue many a large blaze. The tower was purchased in 1924 and the huge mast raised by coil springs could be extended to a height of 65'. The tower nozzle, together with the huge gear controlled deck turret gun could deliver 6,275 gallons of water per minute. The unit was withdrawn from service in 1953.

The first fully enclosed pumping engine in the Detroit Fire Department. Built by the Seagrave Corporation of Columbus, Ohio, this 1,000 gpm twelve cylinder model went into service at Engine 1 in July, 1936. Known as a Model JW-440 T, the unit was one of eight similar sedan type purchased between 1936 and 1937. This same unit was reassigned to Engine 41, and a short time later while connected to a hydrant in fron of the Spitz Furniture Co. fire at Baldwin & Gratiot the pumper was demolished by a falling front wall. This fire occurred on February 27, 195 and this same fire extended to the former station of Engine 20 adjoining the furniture store, burning off the second floor and hose towe Nicknamed the "Pie Wagons", the pioneer units went into service at Engines 11, 13, 18, 20, 21, 22, & 29, soon after they were delivered.

Detroit Department of Street Railways fire hose jumpers. Quickly brought to the scene of a major fire by emergency crews and assembled, the devices permitted the trolley cars to maintain service while the fire was in progress.

A demonstration by the Detroit Fire Department in front of old City Hall in 1941. Firefighters are shown climbing the 100 foot aerial of Ladder Co. 1. The 1937 Seagrave was the first unit to be delivered to the department with a fully enclosed five man cab tractor and all steel main ladder.

Ladder Co. No. 2 - Seagrave 100' all steel aerial ladder truck. One of three such units delivered to the Fire Department. The unit shown was placed in service in May, 1938, had a five man fully enclosed cab and was equipped with pompier ladders and a chemical tank. Truck was Mfg. No. 88800, Dept. No. 651 and cost $19,800. The truck also served Ladder 6 and in 1962 was rebuilt by the Seagrave Corp. with a new design canopy cab tractor and high pressure fog booster tank system. The truck was renumbered Dept. 989 and was assigned to Ladder 12.

A similar unit delivered to Ladder 1 in June, 1937 was wrecked in a collision with a trolley car at Fort & Woodward in 1950. The tractor was demolished and the trailer section was also rebuilt by Seagrave with a new canopy cab tractor.

Built in Detroit, Michigan, by the "General Fire Truck Corp.", this 1942 city service truck was equipped with a five-man cab. The new truck was used to place Ladder 31 in service that same year at Manistique and E. Warren Aves. This was the only one of its type to be purchased and was the very last truck to be purchased by the department to be equipped with a chemical tank and pompier ladders.

The first four wheel, city service type ladder truck to be delivered to Detroit with a canopy cab. This pioneer unit was built by Seagrave in 1945 and featured a 65 foot aerial ladder along with booster tank and two high-pressure hose reels. The truck shown, was the last apparatus to be purchased with the famous, "Buckeye Roto Ray" revolving red warning lights. The unit was declared surplus by the city in 1965 and sold to the Plymouth, Mich. Fire Dept.

This photo taken on a sunny August afternoon in 1967 is the 1950 Seagrave sedan of Engine 59. The unit was in service at 59 until March of 1969 when they received a new Mack diesel pumper. This rig became an extra pumper at the repair shop and was disposed of in early 1976.

1952, Seagrave, 65 foot aerial truck and one of several purchased to fit in some of our smaller ladder houses which would not accommodate the longer tractor drawn types. This truck went into service at Ladder 8, and later reassigned to Ladder 22. The unit shown, was the last conventional hood type to be purchased by the city until 1969, when similar Am. LaFrance ladder trucks were purchased with 100 foot aerials. These units were cab-over-engine types.

One of sixteen similar sedan pumping engines delivered to the department in 1952-3. This factory delivery photo shows one of the newly designed "70th. Anniversary" models with the siren mounted in the nose and wrap-around bumper. The unit shown went into service at Engine Co. No. 5 in the month of August, 1952.

The first four-wheel drive pumper in the Detroit Fire Department and the first engine to be purchased other than a Seagrave since 1931. The huge sedan pumper was built by the F.W.D. Corp. of Clintonville, Wisconsin and was delivered in January, 1960. The unit was powered with a Waukesha 285 h.p. motor and equipped with a 1,000 gpm. Waterous pump. The pumper weighed 17,810 lbs., was Dept. No. 947 and went into service at Engine 6.

This dual purpose fire fighting unit was built by the Seagrave Corp. of Columbus, Ohio and was placed in service on May 29, 1962. The apparatus was purchased to replace the standard pumper of Engine Co. 48, at Bayside & Sanders Ave. in southwest Detroit. The unit was custom built to bolster the fire fighting potential of this company in the event that the drawbridge on Fort Street over the Rouge River would be open at the time of a fire. The $33,000 "Quad." had a 1,000 gpm. pump, 500 gallon booster tank with electric rewind high pressure reels, a life net and full ladder equipment and tools normally carried by both an engine and ladder company.

Engine Co. No. 20 (Baldwin & Gratiot) was deactivated in May, 1940 and was returned to service in the month of June, 1961 as a crash and foam unit at the Detroit City Airport. This photo taken at the airport in 1963 when department officials inspected the new American LaFrance foam unit at the time it was delivered.

The 1,000 gpm. Mack cab-forward triple combination pumping engine of Engine 31. The unit went into service in October, 1963, and was the first Mack to be purchased by the city since 1929. Not only was this unit the first non-sedan type to be purchased since 1936, but featured other items new to the department such as, air-horns, booster tanks mounted on pumpers and electric booster reels.

Action photo of the remote controlled Squrt boom unit mounted on Engine No. 37 in full operation along with Snorkel Co. No. 1 at a second alarm blaze. The fire originated in a vacant former meat processing plant at Leigh and Copeland Aves. on November 2, 1969. This was the first time the Squrt unit was called into service at a multiple alarm fire.

The cab-forward, 100 foot aerial truck being tested by Am. LaFrance engineers prior to being delivered to the Detroit Fire Department. One of four similar aerials delivered to the department in 1969 at a cost of $65,643 each, this unit went in service at Lad. 23.

On March 7, 1969, the Salvation Army Emergency Canteen, and the Department Band joined city and department officials at the ground breaking for the new station of Engine 7 and Ladder 6. The new quarters at Mt. Elliott & E. Lafayette was completed and dedicated on October 8, 1970 and cost $450,000. At the ground breaking, Mayor Jerome P. Cavanagh and Executive Chief Charles J. Quinlan were in attendance.

The Detroit Fire Department demonstrating new fire apparatus at St. John Hospital on October 29, 1969. Shown with the 100 foot aerial ladder fully extended is the new LaFrance ladder truck delivered to Ladder 31 on the same day. Joining in the demonstration were the two newly acquired Mack pumpers of Engines 52 & 58.

Detroit's first aerial-platform ladder truck was this Sutphen apparatus built in Amblin, Ohio. The $91,800, 21 ton vehicle went into service at Ladder 6 (E. Lafayette & Mt. Elliott) on December 8, 1970. The unit was the last piece of apparatus to be purchased by the city in the traditional red color and the telescopic boom could be extended to a height of 85'.

Detroit joined the swing away from the traditional red to lime-yellow fire apparatus for improved night visibility. The Motor City went one step further and painted the upper cab area white. The first to have the new paint scheme was Boat Tender No. 1, rebuilt on a new chassis by the Apparatus Bureau in 1973.

First piece of fire apparatus to be delivered to the Detroit Fire Department in the white over lime-yellow color scheme which was adopted by the department in 1973. Unit shown is a 100' tractor drawn aerial truck with a 300 gallon booster tank, two high pressure reels and was built by the Seagrave Fire Apparatus Division of the F.W.D. Corp. of Clintonville, Wis. The truck was placed in service at Ladder 29 (Coplin n. of Jefferson) on Nov. 26, 1973. The new truck was Dept. #353, was powered by a diesel engine and cost $84,300.

On May 22, 1974, Engine Co. 29 (Solvay & W. Jefferson) received this 1,000 GPM. Ward-LaFrance pumper. The unit was one of three purchased by the city and all were placed in service during May, 1974. The pumpers were equipped with a booster tank, rear mounted reel and powered by a 300 H.P. diesel engine. The two other similar units went in service at Engine 17 (Second & Burroughs) and at Engine 55 (Ashton & Joy Rd.). The Ward LaFrance Co. of Elmira-Heights, N.Y. had the distinction of delivering the first pumper to the Detroit Fire Dept. in the new white over lime-yellow color scheme adopted by the department early in 1963.

This cab-forward beauty is a *first* for the Detroit Fire Department. The sleek 1,000 gpm. Hahn pumper was built in Hamburg, Pennsylvania and went in service at Engine 5 (Cass & Alexanderine) in the month of July, 1975. A similar unit was placed in service at Engine 42 (W. Chicago & Livernois) the same month.

The largest fleet of pumpers to be delivered to the Detroit Fire Department since 1969 was this fleet of seven Ward-LaFrance pumpers delivered on October, 1976. Lined up in front of Headquarters and along side of Detroit's new trolley line they are shown awaiting inspection by city officials. The units were the first to be delivered without electric sirens and bells, air horns and electronic sirens provided the warning system. The new pumpers featured 500 gallon booster tanks, 1,250 GPM. pumping capacity and a high pressure hose reel mounted on top behind the cab. The new rigs were assigned to Engines: 6, 9, 10, 21, 38, 40 & 46.

Another *first* in the Detroit Fire Department was this Seagrave 100 ft. tractor drawn aerial truck. With a price tag of $117,800, this was the first ladder truck to be delivered without the traditional locomotive bell and the first unit to be purchased with an enclosed tillerman's cab offering complete protection and safety. The tiller cab features power-steering, electric windshield wipers, heater and a communication system with the tractor driver. The rear of the tiller cab slides on a track to permit ingress & egress for the driver. Two high-pressure fog booster reels with electric re-wind are mounted along with a tank on the tractor unit. The unit shown was one of three similar units delivered in the month of June, 1977 and went in service at Ladder 8 (Junction & Rogers), this one was Dept. No. 474. Ladder 11 (Milwaukee & Riopelle) received one of the units, Dept. No. 475 and Ladder 1 received the third unit in July, 1977 at Headquarters, Dept. No. 477.

Fire Dog Charlie

FIRE DOG CHARLIE Officially, his name was Firefighter Charlie Dog of Engine 32. A mixture of terrier and hound, Charlie was the last of a vanishing breed in the Detroit Fire Department. Charlie joined the fire department by wandering in hungry one spring day in 1969 while still a pup of seven months. The old fashioned fire dog he was, Charlie would leap aboard the pumper as soon as the alert bell would hit and ride to the fire with the crew. Charlie received a non-duty injury one day in October, 1971 when he was struck by a hit-and-run driver in front of the station at Hart & Jefferson. One of the men rushed him to the vet and Charlie's life was saved, but he lost the sight of one eye. The men at the station chipped in and paid Charlie's medical bills while he was on limited duty. Charlie even had his own department-issued ID card. It listed his height as 16 inches, his hair as brown, and his weight as 35 pounds. A department order in May, 1976 prohibited animals in fire stations and officially retired Charlie along with other faithful dogs in the department. Charlie found a good home with one of the firefighters who occasionally brought him to the engine house to visit old friends.

Engine House No. 11

Engine 11 Reactivated As A Historical Place And Fire Museum
By Clarence C. Woodard
D.F.D. Historian

When Engine 11 was organized on January 1, 1884 as "Steam Fire Engine Co. No. 11", hay was selling for $11.80 per ton, oats at .31¢ a bushel and a horse could be fed for $73.35 per year. Detroit's population at the time was slightly over 75,000, the east boundry of the city was Mt. Elliott Ave. and to the west, 24th St.

Detroit's oldest fire station was built on the old Bloody Run Creek in 1883 on the northwest corner of Gratiot & Grandy Ave. and went in service with a crew of 10 men including the night watchman on January 1, 1884. Their engine was a third-class Silsby, equipped with a 700 GPM rotary pump, and drawn by two horses. The engine was attended by a four-wheeled hose carriage along with a 1,000 feet of hose, also drawn by two horses. Horsepower served the company for 32 years until a new Seagrave pumper arrived in 1916.

The old station house built at a cost of $13,600 including the lot, is the only existing fire department quarters in the city which served the same company for over ninety years and can boast of having had a tower watchman on duty nightly to spot neighborhood fires. The watchman was discontinued in 1896 with the expansion of the fire alarm system. When Standard Time was introduced in 1885, the hour of the day would be struck on the tower bell. However, the 11 o'clock bell was not struck on Sunday as it would interfere with church bells on the Sabbath. The use of the tower bell was discontinued prior to World War I.

In 1916, the station was remodeled at a cost of $9,416. The horse stalls and the original wood flooring and joists on the first level were removed, a new reinforced concrete floor installed, a kitchen added and the company received a new Seagrave gasoline propelled pumping engine. In 1920 a Packard hose wagon was added to run with the engine. The 65 ft. tower was reduced in height during the second World War in order to mount a Chrysler air-raid siren. The tower was used to dry hose until the company was deactivated.

The old hay loft and other nostalgic evidence of the horse era still exist in the old station house. In 1972, Firefighter Robert deCaussin of Engine 11 had an idea that someday when the fire department no longer needed the station it could be preserved as a historical landmark and turned into a museum. Bob deCaussin was the fourth generation of deCaussins to have manned a post at Engine 11 during a span of 89 years. Robert, his father, grandfather and great-grandfather before him. No other city can match this record.

Subsequent to obtaining the approval of the Fire Commissioner's Office and department officials, the department historian undertook the task of submitting a formal application to the Michigan Historical Commission to have Engine 11's station placed on the National Register of Historical Places as a fire department museum. The application was submitted on December 13, 1974 and after an inspection by Commission officials the station house was placed on the State Register of Historical Sites on June 17, 1975.

Engine 11 was placed out of service on January 20, 1975 as a regular fire company after 91 years of continuous service due to budgetary problems and the telegraph instruments were removed from the station. However, the E.M.S. ambulance unit remained in service to provide emergency medical care in the area until April 11, 1977, when they were moved to the newer quarters of ladder 6.

In the month of May, 1976, the keys to the station were turned over to The Box 42 Associates, a very active fire-buffs' organization who volunteered to clean up and make repairs to the old quarters. Numberous Saturdays were spent washing walls, the woodwork, cleaning the floors, patching plaster and painting. (1964 was the last time the building had been painted by the city).

Recently, the Box 42 Associates acquired a 1917 chain drive Seagrave pumping engine on loan from the Detroit Historical Museum. This old pumper was Dept. No. 302 and saw many years of service at both Engine 12 and 58 in its younger days. The unit remained in service as a foam rig until 1947 when it was retired. A similar engine was placed in service at Engine 11 in 1916 during the transition from horse-drawn to motorized equipment. This newly obtained unit now joins the recently restored 1908 Ahrens steamer which has also found a permanent home at Engine 11.

During the month of March, 1977, things really began to happen. The gong, register and department telephone (#211) had been re-installed and some donated furniture moved in. In addition, on March 10th the department historian was notified by the Michigan History Division that the State Historical Preservation Review Board had recommended the station house to be included on the National Register of Historical Places. This action could ultimately lead to matching government funds being available to restore the station the way it was when horsepower was king.

Detroit school students, citizens and other interested groups now will have a Fire Museum where the story of our dedicated fire service can be preserved. The old station will also serve as a center to promote fire safety, stimulate interest by young visitors to seek a career in the fire department and to learn of the newest fire suppression techniques. Yes, Engine 11 has indeed come alive again.

Accidents

This accident involved Ladder Co. No. 16 and a Harper street car at the corner of Helen and Harper. Several firemen were injured in the collision as the truck was responding to a fire in the year 1926. The 1919 Seagrave city service ladder unit was one of four similar units with rear steer tiller. In 1929, all of these units were rebuilt, shortened and the rear steer eliminated. All were sold for scrap in 1952 and this particular truck was Factory Serial No. 21756 and Dept. No. 338.

On August 20, 1936, both Engine 1 and High Pressure 1 were responding to the same alarm when involved in a collision at W. Lafayette & Cass Ave. Engine 1 had left headquarters traveling north on Wayne (Washington Blvd.) to Lafayette and turned west. High Pressure 1 had traveled west on Larned from headquarters to Cass, turned north intending to turn west on Lafayette to the fire. However, Engine 1 had reached the intersection of Cass just ahead of the high pressure truck which collided with the pumper. There were no injuries to the men riding in the pumper but, both crew members of the high pressure truck were seriously injured when thrown from their rig. The accident proved the value of sedan pumpers and the city ordered 67 more similar units up to 1965 when the department switched to cab-forward types.

Two firefighters of Ladder 23 were injured when their 1920 Seagrave city service ladder truck struck this railroad flasher abutment, while only a block from their destination. The accident occurred on E. Warren & The Detroit Terminal Railroad on June 25, 1945 while the company was responding to a fourth-alarm at the Briggs Manufacturing Co. The driver has swerved to avoid hitting a boy riding a bicycle.

Front-top-view of the wrecked sedan pumper of Engine 48 (Bayside & Sanders). This was one of the eight original Seagrave fully-enclosed engines delivered to the department during 1936 and 1937, these early sedans had wood-rib roof construction. The unit shown was first in service at Engine 18 (Mt. Elliott & Sylvester) in May, 1936 and cost $13,015, was later reassigned to Engine 48 in 1952. This accident happened in 1955 while responding to a fire when the rig flipped over in a ditch along Oakwood Blvd. after colliding with an auto. The apparatus was never repaired and was used for spare parts by the Apparatus Bureau.

Two women being rushed to Receiving Hospital, along with five firefighters were injured when this 1954 GMC. rescue truck of Squad 1 tipped over after colliding with a pick-up truck. The accident occurred on W. Lafayette & 14th St. on February 27, 1962. A witness to the accident was the owner of a private ambulance service who rushed to a telephone and called one of their own to transport the two women to the hospital. The five members of the crew received cuts & bruises.

Engine 56 - 1956 Seagrave sedan type 1,000 gpm. pumping engine. On November 9, 1963, at 10:40 PM while responding to a false fire alarm turned in from box 7277, E. Hildale & Moneart Ave. collided with a passenger auto at E. Hildale & Conley Ave. overturning the apparatus. Firefighter Albert J. Booth was killed and another fireman Theodore Andre seriously injured. A 15 year old boy was apprehended and convicted for turning in the alarm as a prank.

The 1953 Seagrave 85 foot aerial truck of Ladder 18 which was involved in a collision with a private school bus on East Seven Mile Rd. The $40,000 ladder truck was originally delivered to Ladder 6 and was Dept. No. 876. In 1971, the truck was re-assigned to Ladder 18 and the mishap happened when the bus driver paused to let the engine go by but, failed to hear or see the truck following and drove the bus in front of the speeding fire ladder truck. This accident, prompted the department to explore the possibility of installing air horns on the truck tractors where they are quartered with another company. The accident happened in 1972 and injured several school children, none serious.

The wreckage of this 1969 Mack pumper of Engine 6 ended up against at light pole at E. Warren and the Chrysler Service Drive. On September 6, 1975, while responding to a gasoline spillage call two firefighters and the Captain were injured when their pumper was rammed in the front cab area by a motorist at the intersection. Both vehicles spun around in a half-circle, with the auto being crushed between a light pole and the engine. The driver of the car sustained head injuries and a fractured arm.

Fire Department Parades In Detroit
By Clarence C. Woodard

Parades are as colorful a part of the history of firefighting in America as Dalmation mascots and red suspenders.

From the earliest days of the volunteers and the bucket brigade, firemen have jumped at the slightest opportunity to march and display the shiny tools of their trade. Parades are still the focal point of the social activities of many fire departments, large and small.

Detroit has been no exception. The recent Detroit Fire Department centennial parade, held on October 7, 1967, brought to mind other occasions, reaching back more than a century, when Detroit's firemen were on review.

The city's first fire department parade took place at four o'clock in the afternoon of April 29, 1830. Proudly drawn up in parade formation on the public wharf was the town's entire fire department—three hand engine companies and a hook and ladder company that was just being formed. Most of the town's population of 2,222 turned out to watch and admire.

Ninety years were to pass before the next major fire service parade was held in Detroit. It was a solemn occasion, on April 10, 1922, when the city's last fire horses were retired. While the horses that pulled the city's last steamer looked on in dismay, Detroit displayed proudly its new Seagrave motor pumpers and a recently-delivered Ahrens-Fox high pressure hose car equipped with two huge monitor nozzles. Forty-five years after its appearance in the 1922 parade, the old Ahrens-Fox hose wagon appeared in the 1967 centennial salute.

While these were the larger parades, there were other public moments in the D. F. D. history worth remembering.

Back in the days of the "old department," parades were major events and eagerly awaited. The volunteers lavished many hours polishing and decorating their engines, each company doing its utmost to outshine the others. The splendidly uniformed firemen displayed banners and torches, flags and silver speaking trumpets. Some companies even festooned their apparatus with flowers and oil paintings.

In the latter half of the 1800's, it was not unusual for a fire company complete with their engine, to travel hundreds of miles to take part in a firemen's parade in another city. In the spring of 1856, for instance, Engine Company No. 23 of the New York City Fire Department visited Detroit as guests of the Detroit Fire Department. Needless to say, they were royally entertained. In the fall of that year, Engine Company No. 5 was chosen to represent Detroit in the great triennial parade of volunteer fire departments of the United Stats, in New York.

Ed Sherlock was foreman of the company, and Isaac S. Dygert assistant foreman. The company was given a rousing sendoff from Detroit, including a testimonial of two baskets of champagne by Mayor O. M. Hyde. George Foote presented the company with a new white cotton hauling rope for their engine.

Reaching Elmira, N.Y., the company had a six-hour layover for making their train connections. What better excuse for a parade? All over the city the Detroit enginemen noticed posters proclaiming "Ned Buntline on the Know-Nothing Question Tonight." They learned that the noted story writer was scheduled to lecture in one of the public halls that night. Just then a somewhat-picturesque gentleman introduced himself to Foreman Sherlock as Ned Buntline and invited the company to follow him. The invitatin was accepted,and under the chaperonage of Mr. Buntline, the Detroiters visited the Mayor of the city, the fire engine houses, and various other places. Thus it happened that author Buntline was a fellow passenger when Detroit Engine Co. 5 resumed its journey to New York — and "Know-Nothingism" was not discussed at Elmira that night.

In New York, the company was gloriously entertained by Engine 23, with Mr. Buntline's aid, and the Detroit crew received many glowing and favorable tributes in newspaper stories.

Detroit's volunteer fire department continued to grow until, in 1859, there were twelve hand engine companies, two hook and ladder companies and two independent hose companies. Parades were held twice a year and were popular with the citizens.

Changes, however, were coming. With the arrival of the city's second steam fire engine, an Amoskeag, in January, 1861, the volunteer companies began to disband.

On June 14th of that year the last of the semi-annual parades of the "old department" was held. Two hand engines, the two steamers, Luckner's Band, the Chief Engineer and his assistants participated, led by the Mayor and Common Council. The last hand engine companies in Detroit were disbanded in February, 1865, upon the arrival of the fourth steam pumper.

The new paid department continued to parade with their equipment on each Independence Day, and on events of the civic importance like the placing of the cornerstone of the new City Hall on August 10, 1868, and the unveiling of the Soldiers and Sailors Monument in Cadillac Square in 1872. For such important occasions the entire department turned out. The last Detroit hand engine to appear in a parade was a relic once used by Lafayette Engine Co. No. 4. Along with the same company's hose reel, this engine appeared in a Fire Prevention parade on October 4, 1921.

Few fire department parades of any note were held in Detroit since 1922. Early in 1967, however, the Fire Prevention Committee of the Greater Detroit Board of Commerce formulated plans for a tribute to the 100th anniversary of the founding of the department to be marked by a huge parade and a Firemen's Ball. Gerald Montgomery, who retired in 1940 after ten years as director of the Detroit Fire Department's public relations bureau, served as chairman and parade marshal. The first order of business for the new committee was to appoint Fire Commissioner Paxton Mendelssohn, the "grand old man" of the Detroit Fire Department, honorary parade marshal. As a tribute to his many years of service to the city and fire department, he rode at the head of the parade.

Right on schedule at 10:00 a.m. on Saturday, October 7th, the greatest parade in the history of the Detroit Fire Department was ready to move off from the new Fisher Freeway service drive (Vernor) and proceed south down Woodward Avenue.

Grown for the 1967 Fire Department Centennial, the handlebar appendages adorning the upper lip of fire fighters Emiel De Smet and Robert Pepper were classic examples of those worn by firemen of another generation.

Detroiters who braved a chill wind were treated to one of the most spectacular displays of antique and modern fire apparatus ever seen in the city.

In preparing for a parade of this magnitude, it took considerable spirited effort by the Fire Chief's Office and Public relations bureau, along with the board of Commerce Fire Prevention Committee, to contact the more than sixty suburban fire departments to invite them to participate. The response was overwhelming, with commitments pouring in from Wayne, Oakland and Macomb counties, and two counties from neighboring Canada to give it an international flavor.

Canada was celebrating the 100th anniversary of its confederation. Essex and Kent Counties were also celebrating the centennials of the founding of their fire services. As a result, the Canadian contingent of more than twenty units were able to furnish most of the older equipment for the Detroit parade.

The Windsor, Ontario, Fire Department sent four pieces of apparatus and a command car. There was a Windsor band in the line of March, and Sarnia, Ontario sent a large float carrying a small replica of a hand engine.

The parade was led by the D. F. D. color and honor guard, along with the honorary parade marshal and senior officers of the department, followed by the Detroit Police Mounted Division. Next came the Detroit

Detroit firefighters pass in review in the great Centennial parade on October 7, 1967.

"Centennial Parade"- The 1923 Ahrens-Fox piston pumper of the Mt. Clemens Volunteer Fire Department Association. Following, is a 1924 America LaFrance chain driven pumper retired from the Birmingham Fire Dept.

Dalmation Club, walking twenty of their traditional firehouse pets. Behind a banner proclaiming "100 Years of Progress in Fire Fighting" came an impressive array of antique and modern fire equipment. There was an 1830 hand-tub pumper from Amherstburg, Ontario, a hand-drawn 1869 hose reel from Tilbury, Ontario, and a refurbished 1867 squirrel-tail hand engine from Bothwell, Ontario. Chatham, Ontario sent a fully-restored Hyslop & Ronald steamer, built in Chatham in 1870 and drawn by four horses, with a full head of steam in its boiler. The Chatham firemen rescued the old engine from the junk heap and restored it, raising money for the project by holding dances and

other special events. The wheels were rebuilt by a Mennonite craftsman near Kitchener, Ontario.

Two Model "T" Ford chemical engines were there, too. One was a 1919 model, from the Wayne County General Hospital, and the other was a 1924 rig loaned by the Detroit Historical Museum.

The old 1928 Seagrave open-cab pumper of Engine 3, retired in 1953, and a 1929 Mack, formerly Engine 10 in Detroit, now in reserve service with the Franklin Village Volunteer Fire Department, were also in the line of march.

Other vintage motor apparatus in the parade included a classic, fully-restored 1923 Ahrens-Fox

Detroit's newest Seagrave 100 foot aerial ladder trucks pass the reviewing stand at Kennedy Square during the 1967 Centennial parade. The units were later assigned to Ladder Companies No. 1 and 17.

piston pumper from Mount Clemens, Michigan; a fully-restored 1924 American-LaFrance Type 75 pumper from Birmingham; a beautifully-restored 1929 Bickle pumper, from Leamington, Ontario, resplendent in its bright red paint and elaborate gold-leaf decoration, and a 1936 LaFrance tractor-drawn aerial ladder truck which was retired from reserve service on the Windsor department the following month.

The Mount Clemens firemen handed out 1,000 roses to spectators along the way. Detroit firefighters, dressed in bright red shirts and suspenders and sporting handsome moustaches grown for the occasion, added a colorful note as they rode each rig.

Modern apparatus from communities for miles around followed the antique machines. Grosse Pointe Woods, for instance, sent their new Seagrave snorkel-pumper.

Bringing up the rear of the parade was a massive array of Detroit's newest apparatus and more than two hundred uniformed, marching firemen. First came the big, 85-foot FWD-Pitman snorkel, two gleaming new Mack diesel pumpers, and two new Seagrave 100-foot tractor-type aerials right out of the workshop where they were being readied for service, made an impressive spectacle as they rolled by, lights flashing. Then came

the 1950 GMC-General fireboat tender, a new squad and the department ambulance.

Civic and fire department dignitaries from many of the departments participating watched the ninety-minute parade from a reviewing stand on Woodward Avenue.

The parade disbanded at Woodward and Congress, and as in the days of the old parades, those taking part were treated to refreshments by their D. F. D. hosts at the Disabled Veterans Hall on East Jefferson at Rivard.

The parade statistics were almost as impressive as the parade itself; a total of sixty-five units took place. More than eight hundred and fifty persons, including one hundred and ten firemen from Detroit and other fire departments who rode on the apparatus, and five hundred and thirty non-firemen made this the greatest firemen's parade in the city's history.

A gala Firemen's Ball in Cobo Hall, highlighted by a midnight appearance by the Detroit fireboat "John Kendall," its fourteen big streams illuminated by searchlights on the Detroit River, brought this memorable day to a close.

It is unlikely that as impressive a spectacle will be held again for some time.

The Rescue Squad

The original "Flying Squadron". Known as Engine Co. No. 30, this four cylinder Packard was the first automobile in the Detroit Fire Dept., as well as the very first auxiliary squad company in the nation. The unit went into service on October 15, 1908.

The Rescue Squad Story
Of The
Detroit Fire Department

Fifteen trained men, possessing the skill of an acrobat and the courage of a "Daniel" were drafted as the original "Flying Squadron", which became the first automobile unit in the Fire Department. The new company known as Engine 30, went into service with a Packard squad car on October 15, 1908. The unit was stationed in the quarters of "Steam Fire Engine Co. No. 2", which was then located on the east side of Hastings Street, between Larned and Congress. Detroit was the first city to adopt the idea and the company eventually became "Rescue No. 1"

The men were selected, not only for experience, but also having shown themselves to be specially suited for this type of work. The members received $80 dollars yearly more salary than a pipeman or ladderman and they were unofficially known as "Squad men". The principal object of forming this company was to render aid to other companies in stretching hose lines, raising ladders, saving lives, etc. The name "Flying Squadron" was well applied when considering the hair raising stunts performed by this able body of men, who had only one thing in mind and that to reach their destination. Is it any wonder that the name "Flying Squadron" was given them? Consider today traveling 60 miles per hour through the loop district and traveling from their quarters at Hastings and Congress Streets to Michigan and Cass Ave. in 46 seconds. This was the enviable record of this daring crew, who practically held life by a single thread every time they responded to an alarm.

During the meal-leaves of the other companies, and at night,

Engine 30 responded to all first alarms from boxes in the high-value district. When the breakfast and mid-day meal-leaves were over the squadron went out of service for three hours and sent all hands to meals, the squad members having only these two meal leaves each day. The extra manpower provided by Engine 30 at night fires, when the other companies were up to full strength, was said to be a factor in holding down the number of multiple alarms during the night hours when large fires were most apt to occur.

These men became the pride of the Department through their wonderful work and it was only a matter of a few weeks of service when Engine 30 was nearly forgotten in name, but was referred to by men in the Department as the "Suicide Squad". Like the old sea captain, these men could spill yarn after yarn of their thrilling adventures and miraculous escape of being a telegraph pole ornament... The auxiliary squadron plan proved so successful in Detroit that a number of fire departments in other cities of the nation soon adopted the idea.

The very first Packard was an extra size model and was purchased in September 1908. The unit cost $4,700, was Mfg. No. 7502, and was assigned Dept. No. 35. The vehicle was powered by a four-cylinder, four-cycle motor with a 5-inch cylinders and a 5½ inch stroke. Was equipped with 36 x 5 inch Morgan & Wright tires, on Continental rims. The headlights were two solar lens mirror search lights, and one extra tire on Continental rim was carried on the left running board. Other equipment carried consisted of three Babcock soda & acid hand extinguishers, one door opener, two axes and one canvas stretcher. A quarter-fold life net was added later and the unit weighed 4,250 pounds when ready for service.

Speeds of over 50 miles per hour were common for these old Packards and the territory covered by Engine 30 was West Jefferson to Clark Ave., on the West, East Jefferson to Field Ave. on the East, and North from the River to High St. (now Vernor). In addition, the entire city was covered by multiple alarms. This original Packard was eventually wrecked in a collision on June 6, 1921, while responding to a fire alarm and sold for scrap.

On October 18, 1910, the second Packard squad car was purchased at a cost of $4,669. This new machine replaced the original Packard at Engine 30 and the original unit was then used to form the second squad company known as Engine 34 and went in service at Cass & Alexanderine Ave. with a ten man crew and shared the quarters with Engine 5. This second Packard has been preserved by fire officials and is now in possession of the Detroit Historical Museum.

In the month of October, 1912, a third Packard squad car was purchased and placed in service as Engine 30, their former second Packard was sent to Engine 34, and the original Packard was used to form a new squad company in the station house of Engine 18, on Mt. Elliot near Sylvester Avenue, and was known as Engine 36. On January 18, 1915, the fourth Packard was delivered to the city and was used to form an additional squad company known as Engine 40, they shared the quarters with Engine Co. 27, Junction & Rogers Avenues.

These squads continued on the original plan until 1918, when one by one, the units became regular pumper companies as the city grew and were eventually replaced by four rescue squads designated as Rescue Squads No. 1, 2, 3 and 4. While the four original rescue squads were, and still are, basically manpower units for fire service, their equipment was augmented to include; modern life-nets, various breathing apparatus, cutting equipment and specialized tools. In 1947, Squad 5 was added, and in 1951, Squads 6 and 7 were organized, the word 'rescue' having been eliminated from the company designation shortly afterwards. On January 8, 1972, another squad company was placed in service at Hart & E. Jefferson and was known as Tactical Mobile Squad (TMS) No. 9. Two months later on March 14, 1972, Tactical Mobile Squad No. 8 was organized at Central & Dix Ave.

One of the nine squads (TMS as they are now being called) responds to all fire alarms by telegraph, another on second alarms, and on many multiple alarms a third squad responds on fourth alarm. On June 19, 1972, the first of 16 Emergency Medical Service units were placed in service with the last one going in service on January 3, 1973. The new civilian ambulances have taken over the "specials" and medical emergencies formerly handled by the squads. The Fire Dept. TMS squads will again only be used as support and rescue units for the firefighters and bonifide calls, like extricating victims from the twisted wreckage of auto accidents or similar assignments.

C. C. Woodard,
D.F.D. Historian

Rescue Co. No. 1, shown with their 1922 Packard squad car. This station house was erected in 1918 and adjoined the quarters of Engine 2 at the N.W. corner of E. Larned & St. Antoine.

The famous squad rig of Rescue 4. Historically, Detroit had used relatively little American LaFrance fire apparatus, relying instead on a large fleet of Seagraves and Ahrens-Foxes. In 1934, however, the department purchased this special American La-France, Series 300 rescue squad car, powered by a 240 H.P. V-12 engine. Note the unusual half-doors on the cab and the louvreless hood. The truck was fully enclosed in 1941 and remained at Rescue 4 until 1948 when it was retired to an extra unit. The squad truck was sold for scrap in 1954, along with most of the Ahrens-Fox pumpers and city service ladder trucks left over from 1920's.

A custom built squad car constructed by the apparatus bureau in 1939. One of two such units built from 1921 Ahrens-Fox aerial truck tractors. A similar unit saw service at squad 3 and both were fully enclosed in 1941 and continued in service until 1944.

1941 Cadillac Squad car, one of two similar units in service at Rescue 2 & 3. The unit shown was taken at Detroit City Airport and was squad 3. Later this same apparatus was assigned to Rescue 4 and while responding to an alarm of fire from the Detroit Lumber Co., this unit collided with a police car driven by a sergeant who was also responding to an emergency call. The accident took place at W. Lafayette & Livernois in 1948 and also took the lives of two members of the fire company, as well as that of the police sergeant.

1949 Squad car of Rescue 1, shown shortly after the company moved to Fire Headquarters. The body was constructed by the Proctor-Keefe Co. of Detroit on a G.M.C. chassis.

A typical Detroit squad company in action. A crew works gingerly to extricate the driver of his overturned semi-truck tractor which had skidded out-of-control and climbed a freeway embankment.

The 1964 squad car of Squad 4. The truck body was manufactured in Wooster, Ohio by the Gerstenslager Co. and mounted on a G.M.C. chassis.

The Detroit Fire Department placed one of these special Tactical Mobile Squads in service at Greenfield & Fenkell in 1973. It was built on a GMC four-wheel drive chassis and was powered by a V-8 gasoline engine. This TMS unit carried booster equipment and 300 gallons of water. The FWD configuration and large flotation tires were designed to enable the unit to climb freeway embankments. The unit was painted lime-yellow and white and had a crew bench behind the cab. The body was built by a local firm. The special rig was difficult to maneuver on city streets and no others were placed in service.

Engine Co. No. 4

This 1969 photograph of the station house of Engine Co. No. 4, located on Eighteenth St. nr. Howard, was the second oldest fire station in Detroit at the time. The building was originally erected in 1897 and remodeled by the department in 1921. This building was only antedated by Engine 11's station at Gratiot & Grandy built in 1883. Engine 4 was placed out of service in 1976.

Fire Department Association

Detroit Volunteer Fire Department

The original "Firemen's Hall". The building was constructed in 1839 on the N.W. corner of East Larned and Bates opposite the present City-County Building.

Our early volunteer fire department by 1838, now consisted of four hand engine and one hook and ladder company. As the firemen increased in number, on August 21, a reading room and library was opened.

In the month of January, 1839, Common Council obtained the use of a lot on the N.W. corner of E. Larned and Bates Street, and on this site the first Firemen's Hall was erected at a cost of $3,300. It was paid for by the city along with funds contributed by the firemen and interested citizens. The new hall provided space for meeting rooms, the library, and served as quarters for the hand engine company "Protection" No. 1; "Hurlbut" Hose Co. No. 1 and "Rescue" Hook and Ladder & Axe Co. No. 1.

On January 11, 1840, The fire department received its first charter from the Legislature under the name of the "Fire Department of the City of Detroit". A meeting was held at Firemen's Hall for the purpose of a permenant organization and James A. Van Dyke was a delegate from Protection Engine Co. No. 1. A constitution and by-laws were drawn setting forth that a thorough and more perfect organization of the department and facilities for the relief and maintenance of disabled and indigent firemen and their families were the object of the organization. The organization was called the "Fire Department Association" and they conducted their business in the original Firemen's Hall.

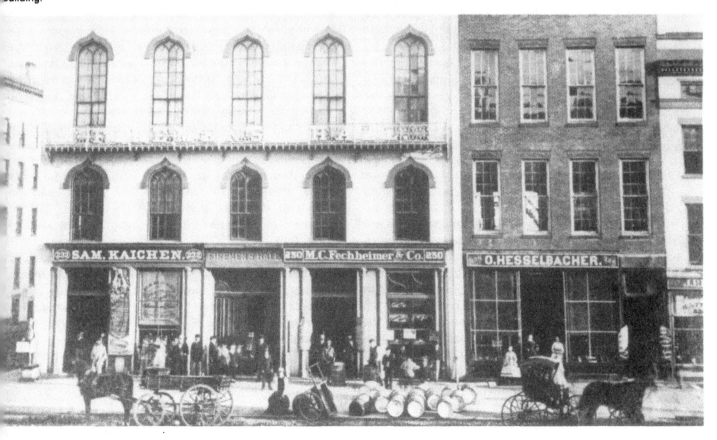

"Firemen's Hall" in 1885, was occupied on the ground floor by Sam Kaichen's tobacco shop complete with wooden Indian and the adjoining wine shop of M. C. Fechheimer & Co.

This Association was formed on Feb. 14, 1840.

Early in 1847, the original hall was found to be insufficient as the number of volunteer fire companies grew and with $6,000 in funds in the treasury it was decided to build a larger Firemen's Hall. In the month of September, 1847, a lot was purchased on the south-west corner of Randolph and E. Jefferson Avenue. A building committee was formed consisting of James Van Dyke, H.B. Le Roy and Hugh Moffat.

Through the efforts of James Van Dyke, a loan of $8,000 was obtained and on June 7, 1850 work began on construction of the new "Firemen's Hall". However, due to increased construction costs and lack of funds, the hall was not completed until January 7, 1853. The cost of the lot was $9,000 and the building $17,000. The new hall was opened with a concert by Theresa Parodi.

The entire debt was paid off by gifts from other fire companies, public spirited citizens, a $1,000 gift from the Great Western, the Lake Shore and the Detroit & Mackinaw Railways. Also, considerable monetary assistance was received from a large art exhibition held by the Ladies of Detroit raising over a $1,000.

The new three story hall became a literary and social center of the city as well as a spacious library and reading room. The auditorium had a seating capacity of 500 and many theatrical companies, concerts and public entertainments were held here.

Firemen's Hall remained the property of the Fire Department Association for 34 years until 1887, at which time the building was sold to the Water Commission. After the sale of the hall the Association had accumulated $100,000 in cash and in 1887 had fulfilled its mission. Each member of the 130 remaining Fire Department Association members were voted $500 in cash, and in addition beds in St. Luke's, Harper and St. Mary's Hospitals were bought and by endowment were made forever free to members of the old volunteer and early paid department. The balance of $20,000 was used to relieve the widows and orphans of former members of the disbanded Association.

By: Clarence C. Woodard

Fireman's Fund

The Detroit Firemen's Fund Association was organized as a non-profit organization on March 16, 1866 and was incorporated on April 13, 1867. The Fund was formed to assist the widows and orphans of Firefighters and to assist Firefighters who have become disabled. The Fund has also purchased and maintains burial plots for Firefighters who express the desire to be interred in close proximity to their firefighting brothers. Each year on Memorial Day, services are held at the cemetery to honor our fallen brothers. The services include a uniformed parade of firefighters, the Department Band, and the Honor Guard of both the V.F.W. and the American Legion. Wreaths are placed and Taps are sounded in an impressive ceremony which in '77 was attended by over 100 firefighters who wished to pay homage.

In order to finance these various services, dues are collected from all members. A Yearbook is issued each year through the donations of local merchants and friends of the Department, and a Field Day is held at tiger Stadium, the home of the Detroit Tigers. The 55th Annual Field Day for 1977, was held on August 21st. The Field Days are financed through the support of the citizens of Detroit and its' environs. This is primarily a display by the Fire Department Thrill Team with demonstrations showing rope slides, the use of the life net, ladder raising and varied other feats. We also have a Clown Team composed entirely of firefighters who perform with expertize at this event. The Clown Team also donates their time year round, to amuse and entertain children in hospitals and orphanages. They give freely of their time in rest homes and nursing homes to alleviate the boredom of our senior citizens. We engage a limited number of professional acts, in '76 we had high wire acts, in previous years we have had the "Human Cannonball" and in 1977 we engaged "Superman", Guy Gibby, who performs feats of strength which includes pulling a car with his teeth. Each year one member of the Department is chosen to receive the "Jefferson Medal of Valor" for what is deemed to be the most heroic act of the year. This presentation is made at the Field Day. The '77 award went to Firefighter Edward Smith III, who is following in the footsteps of his father who is a present battalion chief in the Department.

The Firemen's Fund is composed of nine elected Trustees who serve a three year term, plus an ex-officio member, the Chief of Department. It is the duty of the Trustees to handle the funds of this organization in accordance with the By-Laws, which regulates all financial transactions.

Frederick H.Nicholls
President, Detroit Firemen's Fund

THE CITY OF DETROIT

SPERAMVS MELIORA

RESVRGET CINERIBVS

MICHIGAN

The original seal of the City of Detroit commemorating the great fire which wiped out the frontier village in 1805 was adopted by Common Council on May 10, 1829. "Speramus Meliora" (We hope for better things)- "Resurget Cineribus" (It shall rise again from the ashes). The city seal and motto shown in this photo is the re-designed version by Sculptor Marshall Fredericks in 1956.

Volunteer Fire Department

Chief Engineers Of Detroit's Volunteer Fire Department
By Clarence C. Woodard

On September 25, 1825, Detroit's Common Council appointed and confirmed our first volunteer fire engine company. The new company was known as "Protection No. 1" and David McKinstry was appointed Chief Engineer.

Detroiters owe a debt of gratitude to our valiant pioneer Fire Chiefs, or Chief Engineers as they were called then. These gallant men along with their faithful volunteer firemen, served their city well and without compensation.

It is here, that we pay tribute to our Chief Engineers and their devotion to duty which continued until Common Council formally disbanded all hand engine companies on February 17, 1865:

Name	Years	
1. David McKinstry	1825-29	
2. Levi Cook	1830	
3. J. L. Whiting	1831	
4. Marshal Chapin	1832	
5. Levi Cook (reappointed)	1833-35	
6. Noah Sutton	1835	
7. H. V. Disbrow	1836	
8. Chauncy Hurlbut	1837-41	
9. Matthew Gooding	1842	
10. H. H. Le Roy	1843	
11. James Stewart	1844-46	
12. William Barclay	1847-48	
13. William Duncan	1849-50	
14. L. H. Cobb	1851	
15. John Patton	1852-53	
16. William Duncan (reappointed)	1854-57	
17. William Lee	1858-59	
18. William Holmes	1860	(Jas. Battle was first Asst.)
19. James Battle	1860-62	(first paid fire company in 1860)
20. Thomas Oakley	1863-64	(Jas. Battle was foreman of Eng. 3 during 1863-64)

James Battle
Detroit's First
Fire Chief

Chiefs Of Detroit's Paid Fire Department Since 1865

RANKING	NAME	DATE APPTD.	AGE AT APP'MT.	RETIRED
1st	BATTLE, James	Feb. 7, 1865	34	Feb. 9, 1895
2nd	ELLIOTT, James	Feb. 9, 1895	61	Aug. 31,1898 (Died)
3rd	KENDALL, John	Sept. 16, 1898	59	Jan. 1, 1907
4th	BRODERICK, James C.	Jan. 1, 1907	63	Sept. 1, 1917
5th	MC GRAW, William	Oct. 1, 1917	61	Aug. 8, 1919 (Died)
6th	CALLAHAN, Timothy E.	Sept. 1, 1919	61	Aug. 1, 1925
7th	MEGINNITY, Edward H.	Aug. 1, 1925	66	Mar. 1, 1927
8th	DE MAY, Stephen J.	Mar. 1, 1927	64	Mar. 1, 1932
9th	CALLAHAN, Michael	Mar. 1, 1932	67	Nov. 1, 1932
10th	ISRAEL, Walter F.	Nov. 1, 1932	53	Nov. 1, 1941
11th	THOMPSON, Alexander	Nov. 1, 1941	63	Jan. 1, 1943
12th	KEEFE, John A.	Jan. 1, 1943	61	Oct. 1, 1944
13th	ROURKE, John L.	Oct. 9, 1944	55	Jul. 15, 1946
14th	HIGBY, Ninnian C.	Jul. 22, 1946	54	Jan. 9, 1952
15th	BLOHM, Edward J.	Jan. 10, 1952	59	Jul. 1, 1958
16th	VALLAD, Raymond	Jul. 2, 1958	61	Dec. 30, 1958
17th	ADLER, Joseph H.	Dec. 31, 1958	59	Jul. 1, 1959
18th	DALY, Laurance J.	Jul. 2, 1959	57	Nov. 23, 1962
19th	THOM, Glenn E.	Nov. 24, 1962	56	Jun. 1, 1967
20th	QUINLAN, Charles J.	Jun. 2, 1967	61	May 3, 1970
21st	EMERY, Lester P.	May 4, 1970	58	Aug. 1, 1971
22nd	DENEWETH, Joseph J.	Aug. 2, 1971	57	Dec. 1, 1973
23rd	MOROWSKE, Mahlon C.	Dec. 2, 1973	59	Aug. 1, 1974
24th	DIXON, Samual A.	May 28, 1975	51	June 6, 1975
	(6/6/75 resumed duties as Director of Community Relations)			
25th	ROBINSON, Donald L.	Sept. 2, 1976	45	Oct. 8, 1976
	(10/8/76 resumed duties as Fire Marshal)			
26th	PHILLIPS, Theodore A.	May 26, 1977	59	

CW/MMH

Early Fires
Of Detroit

The Great Fire of Detroit on June 11, 1805, from a painting by Robert Thom.

This photo of "The Detroit Fire - 1805" is one of a series of oil paintings commissioned by the Michigan Bell Telephone Company and completed in 1965. The artist, Robert Thom of Birmingham and widely known for his painstaking attention to detail and historical accuracy spent two months researching data on the fire before he began the painting itself which took a month to complete.

He took note of the city's prevailing wind, the time of day (morning), the kind of household goods and vehicles (two-wheel French carts, four-wheel Yankee carts) in the frontier town at the time. The pathway at the left is Ste. Anne's Street, later to become Jefferson. The fence in the foreground is approximately Randolph Street. At the top, extreme right, is the Fort (where the Federal Building now stands). Between it and the town, which ended at what would now be Larned, was a two-block-long covered way protected by pickets. The artists view is about where the old County Bldg. stands today. At the right is Savoyard Creek. In the center is a cemetery, about where Cadillac Square is now.

Detroit's famous Opera House fire occurred on October 7, 1897 and spread to several adjoining downtown buildings. At the right of the photo smoke can be seen from one of the steam fire engines on Monroe Ave. still working on the ruins.

Steamers in action at Juep Paper Co. third alarm on West Larned at Shelby in February 2, 1901.

Michigan Central Depot Fire . . . . . On December 26, 1913, this spectacular $200,000 blaze destroyed the station at the foot of Third Street. Firefighters rescued nearly 100 newly arrived immigrants from fenced in waiting rooms just prior to the clock tower falling to the street. At the time, the new Michigan Central Depot was under construction and work was rushed to completion.

Chope-Stevens Paper Co. Fire. This huge five-story, 80' x 100' paper warehouse located at 12 E. Woodbridge Ave. corner of Woodward caught fire on July 13, 1914. The blaze was discovered at 2:03 AM and burned for two days before it was extinguished. The aerial ladder truck in the foreground is believed to be Ladder Co. No. 2 which had responded from their station house on E. Larned at St. Antoine.

This 1914 blaze at the Federal Electric Sign System Company went to three alarms before being brought under control. The fire occurred at 63 State St. near Washington Blvd. and shown in the photograph is a mixture of horsepower and gasoline propelled apparatus. In front of the building is an Am LaFrance engine working two lines under a full head of steam and in the far right of the photo is the first water tower purchased in 1893. The rig in the center foreground is the 1910 Webb of Hose Co. No. 1.

Ready to pick-up after an all night battle at the Hugo Scherer multiple alarm blaze on Woodward Ave. in downtown Detroit is Ladder 2. The tall firefighter standing in front of the truck was Walter Callahan. The company had responded from their quarters on E. Larned, east of St. Antoine with this 1918 Seagrave 85′ aerial truck. This truck was the last unit purchased by the department with chain drive and solid rubber tires (other than the water tower). The fire was on January 26, 1920 and Ladder 2 was taken out of service in November, 1951.

The fire boat "James Battle" in action at the Belle Isle Bridge fire. Shortly before 3:00 PM. on April 27, 1915, one of the watchmen on the bridge noticed a blaze in the wood floor timbers caused by hot coals falling from a passing tar wagon and notified the fire department. Although aided by the second fire boat the "James R. Elliott" and several commandeered private boats the firemen fought heroically, but with a brisk wind blowing it was a losing battle and the famed structure was a total loss.

Engines working at the Belle Isle Bridge fire. Shortly before 3:00 pm. on April 27, 1915, a tar wagon crossing the bridge dropped red hot coals several places enroute igniteing the wood floor timbers. Due to a brisk wind blowing from the West the entire structure was destroyed with the exception of one span. Shown in the photo at the corner of Jefferson and the bridge approach from left to right is the Robinson motor pumper of Engine 26 and the LaFrance steamers of Engines 7, 9 & 19. The bridge can be seen burning in the background and on the far right is part of the old amusement center called "Electric Park".

Detroit's Famous Briggs Fire — More than 1,200 men and women were at work in the Briggs Manufacturing Co. Plant at Russell & Harper when an explosion occurred in the spray-painting department. The early morning fire completely destroyed the block long factory on April 23, 1927 and official records listed 21 dead and a fire loss of $2,265,000. This was the first 2-million dollar fire in the city and burned for two days.

This third alarm fire occurred on West Larned St., just East of Shelby and only a block from fire headquarters, on October 24, 1931. The blaze originated in the Felt Belt Co. and spread to other business places in the same building. Shown in the photo is Ladder 1 (1931 Seagrave), Water Tower 1 (1924 Seagrave), High Pressure 1 (1922 Ahrens-Fox) and two Packard hose cars at the curb.

A huge pile of 20,000 cords of wood going up in smoke. This blaze at the Detroit Sulphite Pulp & Paper Co. was one of the most difficult to fight in the department's history. The five alarm fire on W. Jefferson Ave. & Anspatch started on April 27, 1932 and the fire boat John Kendall was on the scene for five days pumping water through 10 lines of 3-inch fire hose.

When Box 178 (Anspach & W. Jefferson) sounded on a windy April afternoon back in 1932, firefighters were greeted by the awesome sight of this huge pile of cord-wood in flames. This aerial photograph taken from the famous Detroit News Autogiro shows Engine 16 (Fire-Boat John Kendall) working turret guns and hand lines from the Zug Island channel. The fire set a Detroit record as it burned for six days despite efforts of the fifth-alarm plus assignment and a heavy rainfall. The loss was set at $248,185.00.

The West side view of the five alarm cord wood fire at the Detroit Sulphite Pulp & Paper Co. at W. Jefferson & Anspatch Ave. The huge blaze occurred on April 27, 1932, when a workman engaged in repairing the overhead conveyor accidentally dropped a gasoline blow torch on the pulp wood piled below. The Fire Department was on the scene for five days.

After an all-night battle at the Michigan Feed & Grain Co. fire on Grand River Ave. at Stanton Ave. on February 7, 1936. Shown are the two first alarm engines locked in and covered by ice from the hose spray on the Grand River Street side. The pumper on the left is the 1929 Mack of Engine 10 and on the right is the 1920 Ahrens-Fox piston pumper of Engine 31.

All the heavy artillery that the department had was in action at this fifth alarm-plus blaze in downtown Detroit. This early morning fire broke out in the five story building occupied by The Advance Glove Co. on May 10, 1937. This action photo taken on W. Jefferson at Griswold shows the high-pressure system in full use. Twenty-seven firefighters are shown manning 16 heavy streams including the deck guns and the water tower. In the fore-ground (from left to right) is High Pressure 1, the water tower, High Pressure 3 and Ladder 1. High pressure 2 was working both 2,000 gpm. deck guns from the Shelby St. side along with several aerial ladder streams at the rear of the building.

The Goodwill Industries fire as seen from the Brush Street side of the large four story building. The fire occurred on March 10, 1938 and required a fifth alarm assignment before it could be brought under control. Note the water tower and aerial ladder pipe in action along with the high pressure system in full operation.

Detroit's Department of Street Railway emergency crew installing trolley car hose jumpers. These portable hose bridges were quickly assembled by the Street Railway in order to maintain street car service when fire hoses were stretched across the tracks. This scene was on Gratiot Ave., looking north on Brush St. at the time of the huge Goodwill Industries fire located at 1453 Brush St., on March 10, 1938.

Detroit's heavy fire fighting artillery in action. This nighttime scene was taken at the fifth alarm blaze at the National Tent & Awning Co. located at 422 W. Jefferson Ave. on April 28, 1938. Shown left to right, the 1937 Seagrave aerial tower of Ladder Co. 1; the 1922 Ahrens-Fox high pressure wagon of High Pressure Co. No. 1, working both deck guns; the 1924 Seagrave water tower with both tower nozzle and deck turret in action and on the extreme right, the 1917 chain drive wagon of High Pressure No. 3 built by Seagrave. Only the front deck gun is in operation.

On June 15, 1939, this fierce five alarm blaze occurred in the abandoned three story factory building formerly occupied by the Gemmer Steering Wheel Co. This photo shows the 16th Street side of the building just prior to the wall falling. The heat was so intense that the crew of Engine 10 was unable to disconnect their 1929 Mack pumper from the hydrant and move same. However, the pumper continued to operate after the steering wheel, seat, and leather wind-breaker was burned off.

The Ray Furniture Store Fire . . . On February 25, 1940, fire broke out in the basement of a restaurant on Michigan Ave. at Livernois. Firefighter Joseph R. Schneider of Ladder 22 lost his life when the floor caved in. The blaze extended to the Ray Furniture store and went to four-alarms. The occupants of the apartments above the stores were carried down ladders through dense smoke and it took firefighters six hours to bring the stubborn $200,000 blaze under control. This view of the Livernois Ave. side of the building shows the crew of Engine 34 working hand lines into the basement. At the extreme right is firefighter Marcena M. Taylor who joined the Fire Department in 1935. Taylor, along with Marvin H. White were the first black firefighters to be hired by the city and both were assigned to Engine 34. Taylor was promoted to Battalion Chief on April 2, 1969.

This five alarm blaze occurred on April 20, 1941 at the Detroit Mill Supply Co., located at 1909 E. Ferry Ave. at Dequindre. Detroit fire-fighters are shown operating from the Grand Trunk Railroad tracks on the West side of the building.

The fire boat John Kendall in action battling a two alarm fire in a gasoline tanker on the Rouge River near the Fort Street Bridge. This blaze occurred on August 8, 1941 and the department was notified when a passerby pulled Box 2347.

Five steam locomotives in their littered stall following the fire at Livernois & Federal. . . A four alarm blaze in the New York Central Railroad roundhouse on December 29, 1942, severely damaged 11 freight and passenger locomotives. Flames shot 100 feet in the air at one time during the spectular fire when the roof caved in. The damage to the locomotives was quickly repaired and they were all returned to service.

The Michigan Steel Casting Co. fire at Atwater & Riopelle Streets on August 27, 1943. Shown in the photo from left-to-right, the 1931 Ahrens-Fox pumper of Engine 9, the 1928 Seagrave of Engine 7 and behind it is the 1922 Ahrens-Fox of Engine 19.

Street car service on Twelfth Street was tied up for several hours as Detroit firemen fought this four alarm basement fire in a super market located at 9310-26 Twelfth Street. This fire occurred on February 20, 1945 and directly in front of the building is the 1930 Seagrave aerial truck of Ladder 15, as well as the 1927 original fire department ambulance after it had been converted to a light and sound truck unit.

Edgar's Sugar House fire, Fourteenth & Bagley Ave., June 3, 1949. Seen in the foreground at this fifth alarm is the 1929 Mack pumper of Engine 10 and the 1937 Seagrave of Ladder 3.

This dramatic photo taken by a photographer from the Craine Studio, shows the Seagrave sedan pumper of Engine 49 at the Grace Harbor Lumber Co. fire in the month of May, 1957. This pumper was one of five similar units of a more streamlined design delivered in 1938. Four other identical 1000 gpm. pumpers went into service at Engines 12, 31, 40 and 50. In 1968, while in extra service, three of these pumpers were assigned to the City Water Dept. to be used for flushing out new water lines during construction of the Lake Huron water intake. During the year 1972, a small community in the U.P. of Michigan by the name of Aura, made an appeal through a Detroit newspaper for a cast off fire engine to help them organize a fire department. In August, of 1972, our city water department, having no further use for one of these pumpers gave the old rig of Engine 31 to the town of Aura.

A dramatic photo of the old Michigan Central Railroad Depot engulfed in fire at Detroit, Michigan. The building of brick and mill construction was built in 1884, and was in the process of being demolished when the fire started. A sudden northerly blast of wind caught fire-fighters by surprise forcing them to flee the sudden burst of heat and smoke leaving behind the 1952 Seagrave sedan pumper of Engine 8 shown at the left of the photograph. The enclosed body of the pumper was destroyed. The block long structure had been used as a freight depot since another serious fire in 1913. The fire was believed to have been started by vagrants who had been sleeping in the building. The fire occurred on June 19, 1966. The pumper was rebuilt with a new body and returned to service in 1967.

The second 5-alarm Detroit warehouse fire in 24 hours roared through this five story brick storage building at E. Larned & Leib Streets. The fire occurred on the morning of June 20, 1966, only hours after the firemen left the scene of the Michigan Central Depot blaze. The fire resulted in two firefighters being injured and the aerial truck of Ladder 10 being damaged by a falling wall. Juveniles were suspected of starting the fire by igniting a pile of rubbish adjoining the building. Detroit's snorkel ladder truck is shown in action at the blaze.

Two firefighters are shown mounting an aerial ladder to place a ladder pipe in action at the Industrial Public Warehouse Co. fire at Atwater & Riopelle on Detroit's east side. The five alarm blaze occurred on July 23, 1968 and completely destroyed the old building of brick and mill construction.

A scene fast becoming rare in Detroit. . . Two Seagrave sedan pumpers working together at a hydrant. These fully enclosed pumping engines were working at a west side multiple alarm when caught by the camera. The first Seagrave safety sedans were delivered to the city in 1936 and the last three in 1965. Over the years 67 Seagraves and one F.W.D. unit were purchased and by 1977 only three remained in regular service.

The dramatic rescue of a Detroit firefighter, John Lisuk at the Vernor-Livernois Bowling Alley fire on October 29, 1968.

Fifth alarm blaze at the former Felician Sisters Academy on St. Aubin Ave. just south of Canfield on November 3, 1969. Note, the effective use of aerial ladder nozzles which contained the fire to upper floors.

A Sad Days Work. . . On March 2, 1970 firefighters from Engine Company 13 found themselves fighting a fire at their former station house at the corner of Russell & East Ferry. The fire which was blamed on a faulty oil heater went to three alarms nearly destroying the 83-year old structure. Engine 13 vacated the station on November 28, 1951 and moved to Milwaukee & Riopelle with Ladder 11. At the time of the fire the building had been rented to the Chapman & Son Tire Company.

The 1969 Am. LaFrance aerial of Ladder Co. 1 getting into action on a bitter cold January day. The fire started in a vacant former hotel building about to be torn down on January 20, 1970. The department was called to the scene late in the afternoon and by the next morning the temperature had dropped to 8 below zero covering the building and apparatus with a heavy coating of ice. The fire occurred at Eight & Fort.

A view of the five alarm blaze in the Dr. Golden Building taken from the Griswold Bldg. The blaze started in the basement of the building and burned through the first floor. A large crowd of spectators were attracted to the scene which started just before the noon lunch hour on April 15, 1970. Apparatus shown on the State St. side of the building from left to right are: Chief 1, Ladders 1 & 3 with aerials raised, directly in front of the ladder trucks is Squad 1 and the fire boat tender directly behind. At the corner of State & Shelby can be seen both Engines 1 & 3 connected to a hydrant and behind Engine 3 is the station wagon of the Deputy Chief and the Medical Unit. The front of Squad 4 can also be seen in the photo. The building was later remodeled and occupied by new tenants.

Actual rescue of an elderly invalid woman by a Detroit firefighter. One of several persons trapped on the fourth floor of a burning apartment building. The three alarm fire occurred on October 26, 1972 in a tenant occupied located at 2258 W. Gd. Boulevard.

Heavy smoke issues from the collapsed roof of Topinka's Country House Restaurant fire at W. Seven Mile Rd., just west of Telegraph Rd. on January 5, 1972. Four alarms were sounded from Box 4775, W. Seven Mile & Telegraph Rd., the first alarm being sent out at 5:21 AM. The building was closed for nearly a year before re-opening for business.

Firemen battling a fifth alarm at the Michigan Abrasive Co. plant in the Eight Mile & Groesbeck area. This fire, on October 19, 1973, was the first time in the history of the Detroit Fire Department that the fire fighting efforts were directed from a Detroit Police helicopter. Deputy Chief Leno Gerometta riding in the helicopter (upper right in photo) was able to warn firefighters about the imminent collapse of a roof on which they were standing.

105

Left: A scene too often repeated among Detroit firefighters. . . Another victim of smoke inhalation. Still groggy from toxic fumes, this fireman is being comforted by his Battalion Chief and a member of his company.

Right: Firefighters making a hasty retreat via an aerial ladder after flames broke through the roof of this west side church. The blaze on October 23, 1974, broke out in the Preston Methodist-Episcopal Church at 1519 23rd Street in the city's Latin-American Community and went to five alarms leveling the structure. The fire was started by vandals and had gained considerable headway before being noticed by residents in the area who telephoned the fire department.

The Usher Oil Service Co. . . . A tanker truck exploded while being loaded causing a chain reaction of explosion in kerosene and oil storage tanks. The blaze broke out in the afternoon of March 28, 1975 at 9010 Roselawn Ave. and extended to the adjoining Candler Roofing Company. Scores of area residents on Roselawn and Cloverlawn were evacuated from their homes as oil from two huge storage tanks spilled out into the streets. To contain the huge fire five alarms were called in plus, 17 extra engines, 5 extra trucks, an extra squad, three foam units and one disaster rig. The department spent 20 hours and 53 minutes on the scene.

Detroit's Fire Boats

Detroit's first fire boat was the "Detroiter", which was built by the Craig Shipbuilding Co. of Toledo, Ohio and commissioned in 1893. The "Detroiter" was originally quartered next to a new brick station house at the foot of Fifth St. and was known as Steam Fire Engine Co. No. 16. Dock space was rented from the Michigan Central Railroad for $1.00 a year. A horse drawn hose wagon with an 80 gallon chemical tank and carrying 1,000 feet of three-inch hose would respond from headquarters at Wayne & Larned Streets to all alarms answered by the fire boat. After nine years of faithful service the boat was rebuilt in Pt. Huron, Mich. with a new steel hull and renamed the "James R. Elliott".

By Clarence Woodard and Walter McCall

With more than 25 miles of waterfront, much of it heavily built up and industrialized, Detroit over the years has required the same type of specialized, marine firefighting services found in the largest seaports of the nation.

Four fire boats have served the Detroit Fire Department with distinction over the past 83 years, and it is virtually certain that a fifth, perhaps different in concept from its predecessors, will be on the department's front line well into the next century.

Detroit's first fireboat was the "Detroiter", which was built by the Craig Shipbuilding Co. of Toledo and commissioned in 1893. The "Detroiter" was quartered next to a new brick station at the foot of Fifth Street and was known as Steam Fire Engine Co. No. 16. Dock space was rented from the Michigan Central Railroad for $1 a year. A horse-drawn hose wagon with an 80-gallon chemical tank and carrying 1,000 feet of three-inch hose would respond from Engine House No. 1 at Wayne and Larned Streets to all alarms answered by the fireboat.

The "Detroiter" was 115 feet long, had a 25-foot beam, nine-foot draft and a hold depth of 10 feet. She had two double engines and tubular boilers. Her two sets of double-acting pumps could throw 15 streams, or the entire discharge could be directed through a swivel nozzle above the pilothouse. She carried 2,000 feet of 3½-inch hose, 2,000 feet of 3-inch hose and 1,000 feet of 2½-inch line on pivoted reels astern. There were three discharge pipes amidships and eight forward. The boat cost $31,765 and was manned by 12 men under the command of Captain Roderick Morrison.

The first major fire the "Detroiter" fought was the Edson Moore & Co. dry goods store fire on November 23, 1893. Seven employees died in the fire which destroyed the six story building and only the big streams supplied by the "Detroiter" confined the flames to the building. The following year, Fire Chief James Battle reported to the Fire Commission that the "Detroiter" had proved its worth during the first year of operation.

The "Detroiter" was retired from active service in 1902 and it was taken to Port Huron where her machinery was removed, rebuilt, and placed in a new steel hull. The new boat was renamed the "James R. Elliott" and returned to Detroit in 1903 to join Detroit's other new fire boat, the "James Battle" in protecting Detroit's sprawling waterfront.

The "James Battle" was launched at the Detroit Shipbuilding Co. yards in Wyandotte on October 13, 1900, and was named after Detroit's first Fire Chief. The "James Battle" went into service on January 15, 1901 and was quartered at the "Detroiter's" old dock at the foot of Fifth St., where it also ran as Steam Fire Engine Co. 16. The new boat's hull and deck house was of steel construction, was 122 feet long, had a beam of 25 feet, an 11-foot draft and a top speed of 14 miles per hour. Her pumps were built by Thomas Manning Jr. Co., of Cleveland. Each pump took suction through a gated connection from a 14-inch pipe extending athwardships. She had two turret pipes on her deckhouse, two stern hose connections, five more on each side and eight on the forward deck. Equipment included 2,000 feet of 3½-inch hose, 2,000 feet of three-inch hose and 1,000 feet of 2½-inch hose.

In 1929, a test of the pumps was made in which each of the two pumps delivered approximately 2,900 gallons per minute at 160 pounds pressure.

In 1936 the "Battle" was equipped with Cummins diesel engines to power her pumps, while retaining steam for propulsion. Yet another new fireboat, the "John Kendall" had been placed in service in February, 1930. The "James Battle" was decommissioned in February, 1940 and the company known as Engine Co. No. 25 was disbanded. In May, 1941 the "Battle" was sold to the Sincennes-McNaughton firm in Montreal, Canada. The boat remained in drydock at Sorel, Que. until November, 1941 when it was sent to break up ice on the Soulange Canal to make way for two American sub-chasers on their way to Montreal from Chicago.

In July, 1942 the "Battle" sailed for Halifax, Nova Scotia where it worked in the harbor for the duration of the war under contract to the National Harbour Board of Canada. In 1945 the "James Battle" went into drydock at Sorel, where it remained for the next 10 years. In 1955 the Sincennes-McNaughton Co. installed a new 1,000-horsepower engine and new superstructure. The rebuilt boat went to work in towing and salvage operations and has sailed to

The fire boat "James Battle" was launched at the Detroit Shipbuilding yards in Wyandotte, Michigan on October 13, 1900, and was named after Detroit's first fire chief. The "James Battle" went into service on January 15, 1901 and was quartered at the "Detroiter's" old dock at the foot of Fifth Street, where it also ran as Steam Fire Engine Co. No. 16. The boat was 122 feet long, had a beam of 25 feet, an 11-foot draft and had a top speed of 14 miles per hour. The boat's hull and deck house was of steel construction and the pumps were built by Thomas Manning Jr. Co. of Cleveland, Ohio.

The "James R. Elliott", rebuilt in 1902 from the original Detroiter and served as Engine Co. No. 25 at the foot of McDougall Ave. until retired from active service in 1930.

Toronto, Chicago, Labrador, Milwaukee and occasionally, Detroit. Seventy-seven years later, in 1977, slick and trim once again, she is still going strong.

The "James R. Elliott", which replaced the original Detroiter, was built by the Jenks Shipbuilding Co. of Port Huron and went into service as Steam Fire Engine Co. No. 25 at the foot of McDougall Avenue in February, 1903. It was named in honor of Detroit's second Fire Chief. She was 122 feet long, had a 25-foot beam and a depth of 12 feet. Her engine was built by Cowles Engineering Co. of Brooklyn, N.Y. and she had Manning pumps. The "Elliott" carried 2,000 feet of 3½-inch hose, 2,000 feet of three-inch hose and 1,000 feet of 2½-inch hose and contained the rebuilt machinery from the original "Detroiter".

On April 11, 1931 the "James R. Elliott" was sold by the city to the Owen Sound Transportation Co. of Owen Sound, Ontario. The "Elliott" was remodeled by the installatin of a new diesel engine, passenger accommodations added and the name was changed to Normac. The Normac was used in Lake Superior and Georgian Bay area passenger service until 1968. In 1969 the Normac was resold to a John Letnik and converted into a gourmet floating restaurant in Toronto, Ontario's waterfront. Tied up at the foot of Yonge Street, the former "Elliott" is now known as "Captain John's Harbour Boat Restaurant". It is interesting to note that two of Detroit's former fire boats — the "James Battle" and the "James R. Elliott", — remain afloat on Canadian waters.

Detroit's fourth fire boat, the "John Kendall", was placed in service in February, 1930. The "Kendall" followed tradition when it was named after Detroit's third Fire Chief. The boat was built by the Toledo Ship Building Co. at a cost of $279,800. The "Kendall" succeeded the "Battle" as Engine 16, and the "Battle" replaced the "Elliott" as Engine 25 (foot of McDougall). The "Elliott" was then retired.

On its first official trip up the Detroit River, the powerful "John Kendall", with state, civic and department dignitaries aboard, successfully broke through 12-inch-thick ice, at six knots. In a test of her steering gear, she was backed full-speed into the ice cakes, with Fire Commissioner C. Hayward Murphey at the wheel.

With the temperature at only 17 degrees, on the return trip she took part in a novel experiment. Still in the ice, her engines were shut down, the stern turret gun atop the tower mast was fitted with a four-inch nozzle tip and directed straight astern. The full power of the pumps was used and the backthrust from this discharge was enough to propel the "Kendall" ahead at four or five knots.

The "John Kendall" was designed by Dean Herbert C. Sadler, Professor of Naval Architecture at the University of Michigan. Her specifications were as follows: length, 135 feet; beam, 29 feet; moulded depth, 15 feet six inches; steel construction with ice-breaking bow; engine, a 950-horsepower, condensing type built by the Toledo Shipbuilding Co., turning a nine-foot, four-bladed propeller giving a speed of 16 miles an hour. The "Kendall's" firefighting gear included two 12-inch, four-stage Manistee Roturbo centrifugal pumps, each direct-connected to a General Electric 800-horsepower, five-stage steam turbine. There were also two six-inch, four-stage Manistee Roturbo pumps, each capable of delivering 500 GPM. direct-connected to G.E. two-stage turbines.

In acceptance tests, the main pumps delivered 12,125 GPM. at 150 pounds pump pressure; 10,640 GPM. at 200 pounds; and 5,747 GPM. at 200 pounds; and 816 GPM. at 300 pounds pump pressure.

The pumps discharged into a well-gated, 12-inch forward loop and an eight-inch aft loop, to which are connected by risers to 16 three-inch gate valves located on the deck house, eight forward and eight aft.

The pumps also supplied five 6,500 GPM. Morse Invincible turret nozzles, each with seven different size tips ranging from 1½ to 4½-inches. There were two turrets on the roof of the pilot house, two on the aft end of the deck house, and one on a tower deck 30 feet above the water line.

Steam for driving the pump turbines and all auxiliary units (bilge pumps, boiler feed pumps, oil transfer, sanitary and circulating pumps, capstans, steering gear and fans) was furnished by two Babcock & Wilcox marine water tube boilers.

The first radio equipment in the Detroit Fire Department (using the call-letters of WKDT) was installed on the "John Kendall" a few

Detroit's famous floating fire station the "John Kendall" which covered 25 miles of shore-line in the city and could attain a maximum speed of 16 knots. The boat was capable of delivering 16,000 gallons of water per minute from 16 three-inch hose lines and five turret guns. Streams from her nozzles could carry 235 feet and the ship carried 6,500 feet of hose and carried foam making equipment. The "Kendall" was capable of breaking ice 14-inches thick. In November, 1976 the Kendall was retired from service and sold to an Alpena salvage operator.

months after the boat went into service. The "Kendall" introduced a new innovation in fire boats — chrome-plated railings, turret nozzles, gates and handles, etc.

After the High Pressure System was discontinued on March 1, 1956, only one Boat Tender responded to all waterfront fire calls with the "John Kendall". Stationed at Headquarters, this unit had two turret nozzles and was built by the General-Detroit Corp. on a GMC. chassis in 1950. Two 1922 reserve Ahrens-Fox Boat Tenders (Nos. 2 & 3) were stored at engine houses near the riverfront and were disposed of in December, 1971, after nearly half a century of service.

In addition to fighting waterfront fires, the "Kendall" could also connect hose lines directly into sprinkler systems in many of the buildings which adjoined the river, as well as the D. & C. steamers while they were tied up at their dock. Special fire boat water mains and hydrants extended several blocks from the waterfront and were able to augment land-based pumpers. Engine 16, as the "Kendall" was listed on the D.F.D. roster, was stationed at the foot of 24th Street just below the famed Ambassador Bridge. From this location she could reach any point on the Detroit River or Rouge River in a matter of minutes.

The "John Kendall" and her spectacular aquatic display was an indispensible part of any important event on the Detroit River, the world's busiest inland waterway. Over the years she had greeted hundreds of important visitors and ships on maiden voyages.

The "Kendall" had battled many big waterfront blazes and made at least two trips to the Canadian side of the river to assist at riverfront fires in neighboring Windsor, Ontario. The most spectacular fire which the "John Kendall" and Boat Tender No. 1 had worked at, in recent years, leveled the huge former Michigan Central Railroad passenger station and freight sheds at the foot of Third Street, on the night of June 19, 1966.

The future of the "Kendall" appeared to be uncertain late in 1971 due to budget problems and a shortage of manpower in the department. With the organization of Tactical Mobile Squad 8 (TMS) on the west side of the city on Janauary 8, 1972, the "Kendall" was taken out of regular service. In the event of an emergency, the boat was to remain available and to be manned by a stand-by marine crew and members of TMS 8. This arrangement was in effect until April 4, 1976 when further budget cuts by the city forced the lay-off of several hundred firefighters and the closing down of 10 fire companies including, Engine 16 the "John Kendall".

The "Kendall's" 46-year career as a fire boat came to an end when on November 30, 1976 it was sold to an Alpena, Michigan marine salvage operator. However, plans have been drawn for a replacement which will probably be smaller but faster and more efficient.

Any discussion of Detroit's fire boats would be incomplete without reference to the sleek, 21-foot "Jet" boat that joined the department on October 9, 1970. A gift from the Louisa St. Clair Chapter of the Daughters of the American Revolution, this light, maneuverable rescue craft has already performed yoeman service along Detroit's busy waterfront.

Detroit's "floating firefighters" have indeed written a proud chapter in the history of the Detroit Fire Department.

Former Detroit floating fire engine still in service in the Montreal, Canada Harbor as both a modern tug boat and auxiliary fire boat. The trim craft shown was originally built in Wyandotte, Michigan for the Detroit Fire Department in 1900 and was named after the city's first fire chief "James Battle". The boat was placed out of service as Engine 25 in February, 1940 and was sold to the Sincennes-McNaughton firm of Montreal, Canada a year later. The Battle received a face-lifting in 1955 to the extent of a new pilot house and a new 1,000 HP. diesel engine, this photo was taken shortly afterwards. In 1959, the boat was purchased by the McAllister Towing & Salvage Co. Ltd. and was still in active service in 1977.

The James R. Elliott after being purchased by the Owen Sound Transportation Co. of Ontario, Canada. The steam engine was replaced by a diesel engine, passenger and automobile accommodations added and the name changed to the "Normac" in honor of Captain Norman McKay president of the line at the time. In 1969, the Normac was sailed to Toronto, Ontario where it has been converted to a floating waterfront luxury restaurant.

The Fire Boat "John Kendall" in mid-stream of the Detroit River. This impressive water display was part of the Detroit Fire Department Centennial Celebration in 1967.

Detroit's newest jet fire boat the "Louisa St. Clair" was placed in service during the month of October, 1970. The craft was donated to the Detroit Fire Department by the Louisa St. Clair Chapter of the D.A.R.

Photo by Maurice A. Gernay

A 1977 view of Captain John's Harbour Boat Restaurant. The former Detroit fire boat the "James R. Elliott", built in 1902 retired in 1931 was purchased by the Owen Sound Transportation Co. Remodeled and renamed the "Normac", the former Elliott saw many years service in Canadian waters until 1969 when it was sold to the present owner. Tied up at the foot of Yonge Street in Toronto, Ontario the former fire boat has been converted to a popular sea food eating place.

Detroit's Civil Disturbance

Detroit firefighters met their greatest challenge in the long hot summer of 1967. What started out to be a routine Saturday night turned into a nightmare, as for the following five days hundreds of fires burned out of control in several sections of the city.

What proved to be the worst riot in the nation's history started on a hot muggy July night. The siege began before dawn on July 23, when police raided a "blind-pig" —(Detroit's term for a speakeasy) on Twelfth Street, near Clairmount, on the northwest side of the city. The raid was routine, but the timing bad. Feelings had been running high between the black community and the virtually all-white police department, and surfaced when rumors spun through the area that police used excessive force in arresting the bar's 70 patrons. Years of submerged hostility unfolded as people spilled into the streets and, joined by outsiders, began the systematic looting and fire bombing of stores along Twelfth Street.

Looting and fires soon spread to other areas of the city and was not completely brought under control until four days later. The Fire Department called back off-duty men at 4:30 P.M. Sunday afternoon and requested the aid of suburban fire departments. A total of 41 departments responded to the urgent call with men and apparatus, some coming from as far away as Flint and Lansing along with neighboring Windsor across the river.

The guns of 2,000 police, 6,800 National Guardsmen and 3,300 U.S. Army paratroopers finally restored order in the nation's fifth largest city. Two Detroit firefighters were among the 42 persons killed, 5,000 Detroiters were left homeless, and 3,500 persons jailed. The combined fire departments responded to 1,427 fires the first four days of the rioting, and property damage was estimated in the millions.

By Alfred Murphy
Fire Dispatcher, Retired

Much has been written on various phases of the 1967 riots. It has been reported chronologically and statistically. Much of the Detroit Fire Department operations have been covered. The purpose of this article is to give the reader some insight in the role of the Communications Division of the Detroit Fire Department during that time.

Fire Dispatch of the Detroit Fire Department is charged with the receipt and dispatch of fire alarms and response of fire equipment for all reasons. Procedures had been set up to cover almost any situation that might arise. The fact that new procedures were inaugurated is not detrimental to the existing system. Riot conditions served to show the depth of Fire Dispatch operations.

The morning of July 23, 1967 was dawning when Fire Dispatch received unofficial reports of trouble on 12th Street. Inquiries to nearby fire companies confirmed looting, crowds, and assembly of a large police force on Herman Kiefer Hospital grounds. Fire Dispatch checked with Police Dispatch for information. Police Dispatch would not admit a riot condition or give any information on the unofficial reports that Fire Dispatch had received.

Shortly after, Box 525-Blaine and 12th — was pulled without any confirming phone calls. The normal response is one Engine Company and one Ladder Company. Fire Dispatch sent full box assignment of 3 Engines, 2 Ladders, 1 Squad and 1 Chief. Alarm was false, but all companies reported riot conditions and harassment on 12th Street. The Executive Chief was notified and he immediately came to Fire Dispatch. The Executive Chief ordered all companies notified by radio to stay out of designated areas unless sent by Fire Dispatch. It may be noted here that the Detroit Fire Department had a Civil Alert Procedure. Due to the lack of official notification, Fire Dispatch had to act first on its own and then on the orders of the Executive Chief.

The morning of July 23 was comparatively quiet. By late afternoon, Fire Dispatch had sent 4 multiple alarms by telegraph signals to the Department. Other fires were as large but were not transmitted, as automatic response had to be handled by Fire Dispatch by phone and radio. In the early afternoon, the Executive Chief ordered the recall of all men on leave signal to be sent out. Large fires and lengthy service showed that relief crews would be needed. This was the first time this signal was used. Again let us note that the Detroit Fire Department had an operating procedure.

As ripples in a pond, the riot situation was rapidly committing most of Detroit's fire fighting equipment. In the late afternoon the Executive Chief ordered Fire Dispatch to call all surrounding communities for fire assistance. Detroit had contracts with some nearby communities to aid them, but none to receive aid. Fire Dispatch executed this order and obtained 56 pieces of fire fighting equipment and manpower from 41 communities. Equipment was sent from as far away as Flint and as nearby as Windsor, Ontario, making it iternational in scope. Fire Dispatch assigned engine house locations for responding aid companies. This assignment was a totally new procedure. As the aiding equipment arrived at locations, they were immediately sent to fires. The recall signal provided Detroit Fire Fighters familiar with their districts to be designated by Fire Dispatch to ride and direct the aiding companies. All Detroit and aiding equipment were used in fire fighting operation. The Executive Chief ordered Fire Dispatch to notify all companies that all types of leaves and furloughs were suspended to insure a manpower pool. Fire Dispatch personnel worked triple and double shifts to dispatch companies and carry out all orders of the Executive Chief.

Fire boxes in the riot area were used so often that the circuits became inoperative. This was caused by run down boxes and wires burned or downed. Late in the evening, of the 23rd, all Fire Department response was from telephone calls and radio orders from the Executive Chief and his subordinate commanding officers. As the night wore on, Detroit companies were returning to quarters for fresh crews.

One of the hundreds of fires which occurred during Detroit's disturbance which started on Sunday afternoon, July 23, 1967. This particular fire in the Nickie's Furniture store at the corner of W. Gd. River and 14t St. was on Tuesday, July 25, and was fought only by the two companies shown. A Detroit ladder company and a mutual aid pumper shown in the background. Note, the National Guardsmen which rode all ladder trucks during the rioting.

Fire Dispatch assigned aiding companies to respond with Detroit companies whenever possible to insure radio contact. Calls from aiding companies regarding relieving their men began to come in. Fire Dispatch arranged for and directed the relief of the aiding companies. Food for Fire Dispatch personnel was provided by a civilian source. As some dispatchers approached 24 hours continuous duty, this was greatly appreciated, as well as civilian, clerical and fire department help in answering telephone calls. As the riot grew in intensity, the Executive Chief was still in the area and in radio contact. He made decisions and issued orders as the situation demanded — recall of men, calling for community aid, suspension of leaves, men not to climb water towers or aerials after dusk, due to snipers. Other orders were: evacuate areas of fire equipment so military and police could sweep area, companies to refrain from entering areas without protection from snipers, and harassment, companies to pick up and leave scene if subjected to snipers and harassment. All these and other orders to come were unprecedented. The wisdom of these decisions by the Executive Chief and their execution by Fire Dispatch were in the highest Fire Department tradition.

The riots continued unabated the afternoon of the 24th. All Detroit and aiding companies were working on fires. Companies came in service only to travel miles to their quarters for relief crews. Efficient dispatching dictated a radical change in procedure. Conditions were near warlike and had to be fought on that basis. Fire Dispatch assigned the fire fighting forces to 3 command posts. Strength of each post was kept fluid. As need arose, companies could be and were moved from one post to another. River Rouge Fire Department covered alarms in the extreme southwest section of Detroit, west of River Rouge. All other alarms were covered by the 3 command posts. One of the original command posts had to be evacuated due to sniper fire.

The other 2 posts covered the city until a new post was set up by Fire Dispatch. One Fire Fighter was killed by sniper fire at the command post that was later evacuated. Another Fire Fighter was fatally injured while fire fighting at the riot's worst time. The personnel at Fire Dispatch feel that the deaths of these two brave men were the great tragedy of the riots. The Governor of Michigan declared a state of emergency and set curfew hours. Personnel of Fire Dispatch, reporting for assignment during curfew traveled at great risk. In one instance, armed police protection and transportation were necessary.

During the riots, all calls of sniping, harassment, fuel, apparatus repair, medical staff aid, and relief of crews, police and military aid were handled by the Detroit Fire Department Radio Station KQA205. The traffic on KQA205 was almost continuous for most of the riots. The Executive Chief was kept abreast of events and he issued orders by this means. The record number of alarms dispatched and radio traffic was logged and recorded in much the usual manner.

Of great assistance to Fire Dispatch was the installation of additional Detroit Fire Department phones at the Command Posts. The phones enabled Fire Dispatch to have an exclusive line for dispatching of companies. Detroit Fire Department response now settled into a pattern. Each command post set up a rotating response roster to insure as much rest for companies as possible. The Executive Chief ordered each unit of Detroit Fire Fighters be given a short relief to visit families and get a respite from their ordeal.

At last came the order from the Executive Chief to disband the command posts and return to normal operation. It was an order gratefully received and joyfully carried out. At the present time, new procedures are being studied. It is hoped that Fire Dispatch will continue to serve the citizens of Detroit and the Detroit Fire Department to the best of their ability.

July 23-26, 1967 — Neighborhoods burn, a block at a time — Free Press Photo

Fire equipment being walked into scene of a fire by our Police Officers.

A Tribute To Paxton Mendlessohn

Saddened by the sudden death of former Fire Commissioner Paxton Mendelssohn on December 29, 1970, Detroit fire fighters lost the best friend they ever had.

Mr. Mendelssohn, millionaire, financier and philanthropist, served on the Fire Commission from 1948 to 1969 and compiled one of the most impressive public records in the history of our City.

"Pax" as he was known to his friends, was the son of Louis Mendelssohn, former Chairman of the Fisher Body Corporation and was a long-time resident of Detroit, living on LaSalle Boulevard.

He was especially credited with giving Detroit one of the nation's most comprehensive fire protection systems. As early as 1922, Mr. Mendelssohn served as Chairman of the Fire Prevention Committee of the Detroit Board of Commerce. As such, he earned for his City, for a number of years, the Grand Award of the U.S. Chamber of Commerce for fire prevention.

Upon his recommendation and urging in the mid-1920's, the City Council adopted an ordinance prohibiting the use of dangerous fireworks. He was also instrumental in a campaign that lowered fire insurance rates in Detroit.

An enthusiastic fire buff for many years, he had been present at hundreds of major Detroit fires, no matter the weather or time of day. In his office on the 19th Floor of the Buhl Building, where he worked as a financier and estate trustee, Mr. Mendelssohn kept a radio that monitored all fire calls. Next to it was a fire alarm register, which recorded all box alarms.

On his desk were two red telephones, connected directly to the Fire Department's dispatcher. Also, similar equipment was duplicated in his home and a two-way radio kept him in touch while driving his automobile.

"Pax" was nationally known for his work in fire prevention, and at his own expense, he visited and studied fire departments in Paris, London, Honolulu, Toronto, Montreal, New York, New Orleans, Boston and Chicago. He was a frequent contributor to fire fighting journals and was a much-in-demand speaker at regional meetings of the nation's fire officials.

As a hobby, which grew out of chasing fire engines when he was a little boy in New York City, no one man has given more of his time, loyalty, devotion and affection to the Detroit Fire Department than Mr. Mendelssohn.

He belonged to many national and state fire protection and prevention organizations, and his knowledge of modern fire fighting methods was second to none.

In 1926, Mr. Mendelssohn was the principal organizer of the "Box 12 Associates of Detroit," consisting of a small group of fire buff friends. The original members were — then Fire Commissioner C. Hayward Murphy, Etheridge J. Bell Moran, Ronald Weaver, William Farrand, Robert Loughead and Robert Green.

Box 12 was sounded without charter or by-laws by a group who liked to go to fires and talk about fires. They took the name "Box 12" from the lowest number fire alarm box at Michigan and Cass Avenues. Today, the group has grown to one of the largest fire buff organizations in the City. Members keep out of the way of firemen, but are always ready and willing to assist firefighters in any way possible when attending extra-alarm fires. They also serve in a public relations capacity at major fires, as they view these fires professionally and help set the uninformed spectators straight when they tend to criticize the firemen's work.

"Pax" is best remembered for the gift of three specially-constructed fire department ambulances, which he presented to the City. All were given in the memory of his Mother, Lydia, whose life was dedicated to the sick and unfortunate with whom she came in contact.

Detroit's first fire department ambulance. The unit was presented to the department in 1927 by Paxton Mendelssohn to serve the needs of distressed firefighters, the unit also served as a first-aid station at multiple alarm fires as well as to dispense hot coffee and food. In 1937, this original Packard ambulance was replaced by a new Cadillac unit by Mr. Mendelssohn. The 1927 ambulance was converted to a light & sound truck by the apparatus bureau and used as such until 1952, when it was retired and sold for scrap.

The second ambulance donated to the Detroit Fire Department by Paxton Mendelssohn. The 1937 Cadillac replaced the original Packard unit and went into service at Fire Headquarters that same year. In 1951, the unit was completely refurbished by Mendelssohn and served the department until 1969, when another new modern medical unit was again presented by Commissioner Mendelssohn.

Placed in service on January 15, 1969 by the Detroit Fire Department was this hospital on wheels. The new medical unit was a gift to the department by Fire Commissioner Paxton Mendelssohn, in memory of his Mother, Lydia. One of the most modern units in the nation for the care of injured and sick firemen the vehicle had a special Gerstenslager body on a General Motors Chassis.

The first ambulance was constructed on a Packard chassis and designed not only to serve the needs of injured firemen, but to serve coffee and doughnuts at extra-alarm fires. This unit was accepted by the City and placed in service on June 7, 1927. This was the second such unit ever to be placed in service for the exclusive use of a fire department in the United States.

He replaced this pioneer unit in 1937 with a new 16-cylinder Cadillac ambulance, equipped with air-conditioning, automatic heating, running water, sterilization, surgical cabinets and two cots.

In 1951, he donated another $20,000.00 to rehabilitate and rebuild the body and interior of the 1937 Cadillac ambulance.

Again, on January 15, 1969, Mendelssohn renewed the memorial to his Mother when he presented the City with a sparkling new mobile medical unit which is virtually "an emergency room on wheels."

It carries complete medical and surgical supplies including an aspirator, and four tanks of oxygen, hot and cold running water, air-conditioning and six litters, two of which can be raised to operating table level. Jerome Cavanagh, then Mayor of Detroit, accepted the vehicle in behalf of the City.

Mr. Mendelssohn was appointed Fire Commissioner in 1948, and it was his work as a Commissioner which ranked him as an exceptional public servant.

Detroit's Fire Department was his special love, but at times he was its sternest critic. At a fire, Mendelssohn never gave a direct order — that was the job of the Chief.

But he observed and kept himself informed as to the Department's skill, performance and need or lack of equipment. This first-hand knowledge enabled him to guide the Department, and he became its official and highly respected spokesman.

Mr. Mendelssohn wrote the Department's Manual of Fire Radio Procedure and was instrumental in seeing that the Department received new equipment each year. Through his efforts, our Fire Department maintained its long standard of being one of the finest and best-equipped in the nation.

Because of his devotion and efficiency, "Pax" always had the admiration of the rank and file fire fighters. During his tenure as Commissioner, a succession of Mayors of varied philosophies found one thing in common — they wanted Mendelssohn to stay on the job. His reappointment was automatic as each new administration took office.

His death marked the end of an era for our Fire Department. We commend him, as he has cited fire fighters so many times in the past, "for devotion to his post, above and beyond the call of duty."

Central Fire Alarm Station

It is any wonder that in the hurry and anxiety fire danger inspired the excited person seldom followed or understood the following complicated instructions pertaining to the use of our first fire alarm telegraph sytem:

1867

DIRECTIONS FOR TELEGRAPH FIRE ALARMS

To sound an Alarm for Fire, first TURN THE INSTRUMENT INTO THE CIRCUIT, which is done by turning the small handle OFF from the button near the centre of the instrument board: this will cause the hammer to sound upon the gong, showing that the instrument is in CIRCUIT, and the line is in working order.

Then with the key at the bottom of the instrument board, sound ten (10), which is an Alarm for Fire, then pause, and then sound the number of the box. THESE MUST BE GIVEN THREE TIMES, IN THE ORDER STATED, as follows: Sound the Alarm . . PAUSE. If the number of the box is 24, sound . . . PAUSE, or if the number of the box is 43, sound . . . PAUSE. The pauses should be about two seconds, or the time in which a person would ordinary count three. Care should be taken that the operation is DISTINCT, and at REGULAR INTERVALS. After sounding the Alarm and number of the box as above directed, wait a few moments, and if it has not been distinctly understood, a call may be made from some other locality for "REPEAT", which is 231, thus, . . PAUSE. This being heard in the instrument, the ALARM AND NUMBER OF THE BOX, must be given again as first directed.

Before locking the box, TURN THE INSTRUMENT OUT OF THE CIRCUIT, by turning the small handle ON to the button near the centre of the instrument board. THIS MUST IN ALL CASES BE DONE, AND IN NO EVENT MUST THE INSTRUMENT BE LEFT IN THE CIRCUIT.

The boxes must not be opened except to send an Alarm for FIRE, and persons who are entrusted with the keys to the boxes are requested to report to the office of The Board of Fire Commissioners when any accident occurs either to the instrument or boxes, or any unauthorized persons are found tampering with them.

FIRE ALARM BOX LOCATIONS - 1867

Box
- 2 City Hall
- 3 Engine 3 Clifford & Griswold
- 4 Engine 4, Eighteenth & Howard
- 5 Engine 5, Alexanderine & Cass
- 6 Engine 1, Wayne & Larned
- 7 Engine 2, St Antoine & Larned
- 8 Second & Woodbridge
- 12 Central Police Station, Woodbridge E. of Woodward.
- 13 St Aubin & Atwater
- 14 E. Jefferson & Dubois
- 15 S. side of E. Jeff. & Elmwood
- 16 Wight St., at Frost's - Woodenware Works.
- 17 Chene & Clinton
- 21 Car Works, Crogan (Monroe) St.
- 22 Russell & Croghan (Monroe) St.
- 23 Rivard & Atwater
- 24 Crogan (Monroe) & St Antoine
- 25 Randolph & Gratiot
- 26 Gratiot & St Antoine
- 27 Rivard & Gratiot
- 31 Riopelle & Maple
- 32 Gratiot & Dequindre
- 33 Engine 6, Hastings & High - (Vernor).
- 34 House of Correction, Russell
- 37 Woodward opposite St. John's Church
- 41 Cass & Sibley
- 42 Gd. River & Middle
- 43 Gd. River & Third
- 45 Gd. River & Seventh (Brooklyn)
- 46 Seventh & Locust (Brooklyn & Henry)
- 47 National & Locust (Henry)
- 51 Thompson (Twelfth) & Michigan
- 52 La Salle (16th) & Michigan
- 53 Trowbridge (17th) & Stephen (Bagley)
- 54 First & Michigan
- 56 Fourth & Porter
- 57 Abbott & Seventh (Brooklyn)
- 61 Thompson (Twelfth) & Abbott
- 62 Fort & Eleventh
- 63 Stanton & River Road (West Jefferson)
- 64 Lafferty & River Rd. (West Jefferson)
- 65 Richardson's Match Factory
- 67 Fifth & Woodbridge, Jackson & Wiley-Foundry
- 68 Trumbull & Baker (Bagley)
- 71 Woodward & Larned
- 72 E. Jefferson & Brush
- 121 Fire Commissioner's Office, Fire Headquarters, Wayne & Larned.

It was in 1868 that work was begun on the new Gamewell fire alarm system which was simple to operate and proved to be the first successful alarm system in our city. New gongs were installed in all the engine houses and the original wooden boxes were replaced with new cast iron ones. The new alarm boxes featured a spring wound mechanism which when actuated, would cause a character wheel notched to represent the number of the box to operate, which in turn would send in a telegraphic impulse to all engine houses. Certain fire companies would then respond to the box as assigned in their running book. An alarm could now be transmitted by the simple operation of obtaining the key to the box from a nearby merchant or resident, and upon opening the door, merely pull down a hook-lever. The door to each box was also provided with a trap lock, by which a key, once inserted and turned in the keyhole, could not be released except by means of another key carried by the fire company. Consequently, any person sounding a needless alarm could be identified. The address of local key holders was painted on the back of each alarm box, and as all keys were

---

DETROIT'S EARLY FIRE ALARM SYSTEM
By Clarence C. Woodard

The alarm of "Fire" is age-old. Before primitive man learned to use fire for more than heat and light, he sometimes had to call to others of his group to help him fight it. What a long trail of progress from the cavemen's call to the little red box on the corner, the telephone, the radio! For thousands of years that wild cry of alarm. Then for other ages, and even now in far-away places, the beat of a drum, the blast of a horn or the clang of a bell-then today, the marvelous electrical courier carrying the call for help straight to those who are ready to respond.

In the larger cities much had been done before the advent of the little red box, in the way of broadcasting the alarm of fire. City fathers had long before found it necessary to provide protection-water buckets, ladders and hand pumps-and then they set about devising ways and means for calling out this help with the least possible delay.

Our first fire alarm system dates back to 1827, when the Common council of the City of Detroit purchased a steel triangle gong for giving fire alarms. The gong was fashioned by bending a 4-inch steel bar into a triangle. It weighed about two tons and was eight feet high. A Lewis Davenport was paid the sum of $12.00 for ringing the gong, and could possibly have been the first paid fire department employee in our city. The triangle remained in fire service for many years. When it finally retired from fire service, it was moved to Belle Isle where it was used for a curfew before the present bridge was built. It could be heard all over the island, and those who did not leave at once were stranded when the old bridge was swung open for the night. It finally found its way out to Greenfield Village Museum where it is now on display.

By 1836 the Council provided for paying five dollars to the person first giving an alarm and ringing the gong. There were also very stiff penalties for giving a false alarm.

In 1847 the city was divided into districts by the Council, and the first fire watch was established in the bell tower of the First Presbyterian Church, located at Woodward and Larned Avenues. Fire signals were tapped out from this location until the church burned down on March 25, 1854. (church was rebuilt in 1855 at Gratiot and Farmer).

By 1858, our city had twelve hand engine companies and one hook and ladder company. Watches were established in other church towers and in the cupola of the National Hotel (site now occupied by the First National Building). The hand engines were assigned to two running districts for the first alarm. In 1866, the city had been divided into five fire districts, and two companies were designed to respond to alarms from each district.

When the city grew too large for the old system, watch towers were established in the City Hall and in several engine houses throughout the city. Men were stationed at these towers 24 hours a day. When the man on watch at night noticed a reflection in the sky, he would notify the nearest fire company and tell them the direction of the blaze. One of these tower watchman was John Adameke, known as old "Eagle Eye". While on watch at Engine Co. No. 15, Hubbard and Fort Streets, he spotted a fire, and calling down through the speaking tube to the man on watch below, he reported the fire at Michigan and Washington Blvd. The companies responded and worked on what proved to be a third alarm fire in the old Banner Laundry. The original chair used by the watchman in the tower of old City Hall is now in the possession of the Detroit Historical Museum.

In October, 1866, our city contracted for a fire alarm telegraph system. It was known as the key and bell method and was installed in 49 crude wooden boxes at a cost of $5,700. On January 4, 1867, Detroit's first telegraph fire alarm system was tested and accepted by the city. The first fire bell connected to the new system was in the tower of the First Presbyterian Church at Gratiot and Farmer Streets. Detroit had five steam fire engine companies and one hook and ladder at this time.

On March 27, 1867, The Michigan State Legislature passed Act 453 creating the "Board of Fire Commissioners". The Act gave the Commission "all the power and authority conferred upon or possessed by any and all persons in the City of Detroit for the prevention and extinguishment of fires". One of the first acts of the new Commission was to appoint William J. Wolfe, first Superintendent of Telegraph and Supply Agent and a Frank C. Chambers, bell ringer. Mr. Wolfe's yearly salary was $1,400. The system had less than 20 miles of wire which suspended over roof tops, trees and crude poles. The wooden boxes contained a telegraph key which could be switched into the circuit and the alarm tapped out on it. Directions were widely posted and distributed, but in spite of this precaution, alarms transmitted by excited citizens were often confusing and ambiguous. Weak signals, short circuits, wind storms, sleet and ice plagued the system. During the first year of operation, 191 fires were reported over the new system, and the fire loss was $239,006. The total number of men in the department was 79.

Detroit's Central Fire Alarm Office. The building was erected in 1920 at a cost of $171,034 on city owned land at the corner of Hastings (now Chrysler Freeway) & Macomb Street. The building was still being used as a fire department communications center in 1973 and adjoined Receiving (Detroit General) Hospital.

This 1965 photo shows the second floor nerve center of Central Fire Alarm Office. Detroit's first workable fire alarm system was installed by the Gamewell Co. and was placed in service on November 9, 1870. Radio was introduced in 1929 and by February, 1952 the department was completely equipped with two-way radio in all apparatus.

numbered, their owners were on record by the fire department.

The new system was installed under the able direction of Mark A. Gascoigne and completed in 1870. Mr. Gascoigne, after seven years as foreman of Engine Co. No. 1 and a few months as supply agent, was appointed to this duty. He entered the department in 1853 as a volunteer, fireman, promoted to district engineer in 1869, assistant chief engineer in 1883 and died on January 18, 1885, a victim of loyal devotion to duty.

Upon completion of the new alarm system, the office of "Bell Ringer" was abolished and Frank C. Chambers was dropped from the service. In 1872, an electric bell striker was installed in the new City Hall tower at a cost of $1,800, and a fire watch was established.

As our city continued to grow in 1884, the fire alarm telegraph system now consisted of 151 alarm boxes and 227 miles of overhead wire. The fire fighting force of the city totaled 216 officers and men, eleven steam fire engines, three chemical engines, four hook and ladder trucks, one protective wagon and two supply wagons. The department was still under the command of our first Fire Chief, James R. Battle. During the year 1884, 338 fire alarms were received by the department, and the fire loss was $306,302. Of the 338 alarms received during the year, the method of reporting them is hereby listed:

248 were box alarms, 10 of which were false.

45 reported by the watchman located in the City Hall tower.

21 were reported by telephone.

14 were reported by watchmen stationed in engine house towers. (Watches were maintained in Engine Companies 4, 5, 6, 7, 9, 10, and 11.)

6 were reported to fire sttions by citizens.

4 alarms by the District Telegraph Co. (A.D.T. Co.)

As the original successful alarm system was connected directly to the various fire houses, by 1885, our fire alarm system had to be expanded in keeping with the continued growth of the city. The Fire Commission found it necessary to erect a suitable building to house the system as well as employ a full time operator. During the same year, a new three-story building was erected at 189-191 East Larned Street, between St Antoine and Hastings, to accomodate the new Central Office Fire Alarm Telegraph. The first floor contained the repair shop and stable, the second floor the telegraph office and on the third floor, sleeping quarters. The duty of the operator was to watch for any breaks or interruptions to the telegraph lines.

The successor to Mr. Gascoigne was William J. Gardiner, who, under the tuition of his father, Professor Gardiner, the eminent electrician, began his career as an employee of the Gamewell Co., which was founded by his father. In 1882, Mr. Gardiner was appointed an assistant to Mr. Gascoigne and succeeded him as head of the bureau in 1885. As his assistant, Mr. Gardiner was fortunate in having the services of Louis Gascoigne, son of the late superintendent. Young Gascoigne was 23 years of age at the time and a University of Michigan graduate. Because of his technical training, he was appointed assistant superintendent of the signal bureau. At the time, Detroit had a population of 75,000. The east boundry of the city was Mt. Elliott Ave. and the west boundry, 24th Street.

When standard time was introduced in 1885, the hour of the day was ordered struck on the engine house tower bells. The 11 o'clock bell was not struck on Sunday as it would interfere with church bells on the Sabbath.

Shortly after 1885, the latest Gamewell receiving and transmitting apparatus was installed in the new Central Office and the system was gradually placed on an operation basis similar to our present modern telegraph bureau. Direct contact to the tower watchmen and the engine houses by a new telephone switchboard and telegraph system was now a reality. The Common Council passed a resolution in 1886, requiring fire alarm lines to be placed in underground cable in the downtown area. The project was completed in 1888.

All fire alarms were received over the 17 inch gongs in each station house, resulting in the horses becoming extremely nervous and disturbed when the large gong would sound. The Fire Commission ordered a small tapper bell installed in all engine houses in 1891. Only in the event that the alarm was a "go" would the large bell be switched on by the man on watch.

In 1892, the first keyless fire alarm boxes were installed in the downtown area to reduce the delay in sounding the alarm. Also this same year a reward was offered by the Fire Commission for the apprehension of any person sounding a false alarm. In 1894, the system of automatic transmission of alarms to engine houses was changed to a manual system at a cost of $15,000. The alarm system had now expanded to 22 circuits and 382 fire alarm boxes.

The custom of maintaining a tower watchman in each engine house was abolished in 1896. These watchmen were on duty from 9 p.m. to 6 a.m. daily and were paid a salary of $35.00 per month. However, all fire alarms were still being struck on the City Hall tower bell.

By 1900, with a population of 285,704, the alarm system grew to 423 boxes, and the city now had 476 paid firemen. Also in 1900, the Fire Commission ordered glass installed over the door key in most of the alarm boxes to discourage false alarms.

Louis Gascoigne became superintendent of the bureau in 1902, succeeding Mr. Gardiner. A recognized authority in his chosen vocation, our present alarm system and Central Fire Alarm Headquarters, built in 1920 and located at Hastings and Clinton Streets are monuments to his foresight and careful planning. Mr. Gascoigne retired in 1939 after completing 54 years service in the bureau, he was 77 years of age at the time.

On April 10, 1922, the department was now completely motorized and the engine house bells were ordered to be kept on the "on" position at all times. Consequently, the men would have to "hit the floor" until 8 pm. and after that time "pounce out of bed and climb into their boots" during the night hours.

After thirteen years under the old method, the men were beginning to show extreme physical strain as a result of the large bell ringing constantly as alarms became more frequent. The Board of Fire Commissioners again ordered the small tapper-bell system to be re-installed. The decision "paid off" as the firemen now would "get out" faster, because when they heard the large bell strike, they knew it was a "go". This method is still in use today.

In 1929, the first fire department radio was installed. A one-way transmitter was placed in the central fire alarm office, and a receiver in the newly commissioned fire boat, "John Kendall". The station used the call letters WKDT operating on 1596 kilowatts and 1879 meters. Sixteen years later, in 1945, modern two-way radios were installed in the cars of the Fire Commissioners, and as funds became available, they were installed in all fire apparatus and department vehicles. By February, 1952, the last two engine companies, 47 & 60, were equipped, and the installation task was now completed providing direct communication between all apparatus and Central Office.

Emergency Medical Service

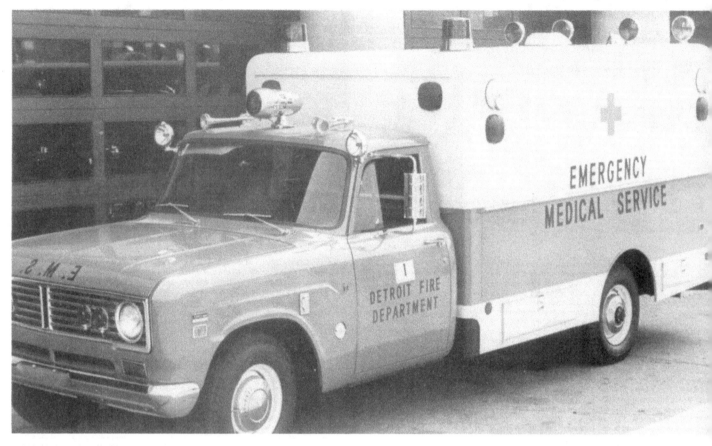

One of Detroit's first Emergency Medical Service Ambulances. Painted a combination of white and bright orange, the units were mounted on a specialized International Harvester 1310 chassis powered by a 197 horsepower engine. The steel construction patient compartment had 60-inches of headroom, were 11 1/2 feet long and was of the replaceable lift on, lift-off type. Assigned to Medic 1 at Bryon & Taylor and sharing quarters with Engine 39, this first unit went in service on June 19, 1972.

The Emergency Medical Service Division (E.M.S.) of the Detroit Fire Department first provided service to our city in June, 1972. Prior to 1972, the emergency medical function had been addressed by Fire Rescue Squads and Police Station wagons.

The formation of E.M.S. had a two pronged objective. First it was recognized that a single, dedicated by function, division would be capable of devoting the manpower and equipment necessary to meet the increased demand for medical care in Detroit. Secondly, it was believed that the E.M.S. Division would release Firefighters and Police Officers from the emergency medical function, and thereby allow them to address their main function of firefighting and law enforcement. These two goals have been realized.

Our short five year history has proven to be exciting, interesting, rewarding, and as can be expected with any emergency service, sometimes frustrating.

I say exciting because of the intensely emergent nature of the work. The interface with Firefighters and Police Officers. The speed and professionalism of working together to achieve the common goal of saving lives.

E.M.S. has proven to be especially rewarding. Each and every member of the Emergency Medical Service can relate many cases in which he or she felt rewarded by the results of their efforts. For example, the mother who is terrified by the sight of her child, battered and bloodied in an auto accident, and who is then gratified and relieved that the quick action of Detroit medics saved the child's life. In a case like this, the kudos from the family, the paycheck from Headquarters, or the departmental citation cannot begin to equal the satisfaction of knowing that competent action saved a person's life.

There are times when emergency operations prove frustrating. Even an experienced veteran cannot help but feel some pain when he or she has been unable to hold off death. We can, however, take comfort in the knowledge that we will continue to strive to improve operations so that as technology and training increase, so does the chance of frustration decrease. We pledge ourselves to this task.

Chief, Daniel J. Bojalad

Captain Marvin White

Battalion Chief Marcena W. Taylor

On April 8, 1969, The Board of Fire Commissioners appointed the first Black Battalion Chief in the history of the Detroit Fire Department.

Two men, Marcena W. Taylor and Marvin White, joined the department as probationary firefighters on April 25, 1938. Having successfully completed their training both men reported for duty at Engine Co. 34, Livernois and Majestic, on the morning of July 30, 1938, to become Detroit's first black firefighters. Marvin White rose to the rank of captain and become the Fire Department Architect, Assistant to the Fire Marshal. (Captain White's career was cut short when he died of natural causes.)

Chief Taylor came to Detroit with his family from Chattanooga, Tennessee in 1916 and attended Detroit Public Schools. He received a Bachelor of Arts degree from Livingston College in North Carolina with a major in Sociology and an English minor. Taylor taught high school English following graduation in North Carolina. Due to illness in the family, he returned to Detroit. This was in 1938 during the depression years when work was difficult to find. He gained employment at the U.S. Post Office, planning to attend graduate school in social work. However, he applied for and was qualified for the Fire Department.

Battalion Chief Taylor now retired, was promoted to sergeant in December, 1952, advanced to lieutenant in July, 1957, and was made captain in November, 1963. Chief Taylor often said, "Despite the rough years when he first came on the job, he enjoyed the work so much he'd do it all over again."

Also, for the first time in the history of the Detroit Fire Department blacks outnumbered whites in a graduating class at the Training Academy on March 4, 1973. Of the 75 men graduated, 43 were black and 32 white. At the time, there were 158 blacks on the department roster of 1,723 men—9.1 percent.

Fire Headquarters Buildings

Old Washington Market building, N.E. Corner Washington and Larned, pictured in its later use as a volunteer fire station. The Berthelet Market was similar in appearance.

The original building on the site of our present Fire Headquarters was the Washington Market Building on Wayne Street, just north of W. Larned and was erected in 1835. The two-story frame structure was one of three Market Places in the heart of Detroit's business area at the time. Each year the city rented stalls to retailers and paid for market clerks and maintenance expenses.

In November, 1842, the Washington Market was closed and the building was outfitted as a school being used as such until 1847. Between 1847 and 1856, the building was again used as a Market Place and operated by local merchants.

The first use of the Wayne and Larned corner by the Fire Department was in 1852 when Volunteer "Rescue" Hook and Ladder Company No. 1 occupied a small building adjoining the Washington Market. The company had moved there from their former quarters in the original Firemen's Hall at Bates and E. Larned.

In 1856, an additional lot was purchased by the city of Wayne Street north of Larned and the Washington Market Building was razed. A new fire station was erected on the site featuring a 65 foot watchman's tower and housed a hand engine company and a hose company.

1857 photo of the first Wayne Street engine house (the two-story structure adjoining the watch tower). The building and tower was built in 1856 next to the existing "Rescue" Hook & Ladder house constructed in 1852 and fronting on Larned St. Originally built for a hand engine and hose company, the two-story building became the quarters of our first paid steam fire company known as, "Lafayette" Steam Fire Engine Co. No. 1.

FIRST HEADQUARTERS BUILDING

On October 4, 1860, Detroit's first paid fire company was organized as, "Lafayette" Steam Fire Engine Company 1 and along with a hose company moved into the Wayne Street Station House. Ten years later in 1870, the one-story hook and ladder house on the corner was razed and a new two-story building erected on the corner to house the ladder company. The adjoining Wayne Street engine house was remodeled and the watch tower rebuilt at the same time.

This new substantial building became our first Headquarters Building with offices being provided for the Commissioners, Secretary, Chief Engineers, The Fire Alarm Telegraph Room and the Superintendent. The cost of the new addition and repairs to the adjoining engine house was in the amount of $11,337.34. The newly remodeled complex served as quarters for a steam fire engine company and a hose company, a ladder company, the Chief Engineer's buggy and a supply wagon. "Chemical Company No. 1" was organized here in the month of October, 1876.

An early Silas Farmer woodcut showing the first Fire Headquarters. The building at the extreme left is the Wayne Street engine house and watch tower built in 1956 which replaced the Washington Market Building. This structure housed Detroit's first steam fire engine and paid fire company in 1860. The addition extending to the corner of Larned with the mansard roof was the new addition built in 1870 to house the "Rescue" Hook and Ladder Co., the Fire Commission, office of the Chief Engineer and the fire alarm office. The entire structure was razed in 1889 and replaced by a second headquarters building. Note the maze of telephone wires overhead prior to the underground cable system.

SECOND HEADQUARTERS BUILDING

The first Headquarters Building served the needs of the Fire Department until 1887 when the building was razed to make way for a newer and larger structure completed in 1888. The new building provided more

When the original headquarters building at W. Larned & Wayne Streets was razed, this second and larger building was erected on the site in 1889 and served as central fire headquarters until 1925, when this building was removed to make way for present fire headquarters which was completed in 1928.

Detroit's Central Fire Headquarters located at W. Larned & Wayne St. (Washington Blvd.). Designed by Hans Gehrke and erected in 1928, the masonry and steel building replaced a former headquarters building constructed in 1889. Total cost including land was $587,900.

INSIDE FIRE HEADQUARTERS - 1939
Left to right
Eng. 1 - 1936 Seagrave sedan pumper, the first one to be purchased by the department.
Lad. 1 - 1937 Seagrave 100' aerial, Detroit's first fully enclosed tractor cab and all-steel aerial section.
W.T. 1 - 1924 Seagrave 65' water tower with deck gun, unit was retired in 1953.
H.P. 1 - 1922 Ahrens-Fox hose wagon with two deck guns, was on dept. roster 49 years.
1938 Buick sedan, Chief of Dept.
1937 Chevrolet, Chief of First Battalion.
1938 Buick sedan, Asst. Chief of Dept.
1937 Cadillac, Dept. Ambulance

(Between 1958 and 1960 every pumper and ladder truck in the department was a Seagrave)

suitable accommodations for both the fire horses and the men. When the original Headquarters was razed the Fire Alarm Office was moved to a three story building on the north side of E. Larned Street, just east of St. Antoine. Later this building served as the quarters of Ladder Company No. 2 until they went out of service in November, 1951.

This second Headquarters served the department during the transition from gas lights to electricity and from horse power to gasoline motors. However, as the horses faded from the scene the building had outlived its usefulness even to the extent of being declared a fire hazard and unsuitable to house the new gasoline motor apparatus. The Fire Commission aware of the need of more land to serve the expanding needs of the Fire Department ordered the purchase of three additional lots on Larned Street in the direction of Shelby to provide for a total frontage of 128 feet.

THIRD HEADQUARTERS BUILDING

Early in 1927, a contract was made with Mr. Hans Gehrke, Detroit's famous architect to draw up plans for a new Headquarters. However, money difficulties were encountered when part of the necessary funds to finance the new building was tied up in litigation, part of the funds were to come from the sale of the former Engine House 3 at Clifford and Griswold Streets. However, there was a question over the validity of the title but the matter was settled out of court and construction was assured. The second Headquarters Building was torn down in 1928, and the present Headquarters was completed and occupied on August 1, 1929 at a cost of $587,900 including the additional land. The new building featured several innovations uncommon to central fire station design at the time; they were, underground parking facilities, a medical division patterned after the one in New York's Headquarters and an auditorium on the fourth floor. The new building housed along with administrative offices, Engine, Ladder, High Pressure and Water Tower No. 1, The Chief and Assistant Chief of Department, Deputy Chief 1 of the downtown district, Battalion Chief 1 and the Fire Marshall's car.

At the time the building was completed, John C. Lodge was Mayor of Detroit. The Board of Fire Commissioners Consisted of:

George W. Trendle, President
Charles F. Cliffert, Vice President
A. A. Schantz, Commissioner
C. Hayward Murphy
Harry Brabyn, Secretary

Stephen J. DeMay was Chief of Department and Wm. M. Burgess, was Chief of Buildings and Grounds.

Today, the present Headquarters is still regarded as a Architectural Classic by City Historians and may someday become an Historical Site.

(NOTE, Wayne Street was changed to Washington Blvd. on May 21, 1959) Wayne Street was relocated to a short two-block stretch behind Cobo Hall afterwards.

Detroit's Famous Fires

On a hill at the foot of Shelby and Griswold streets, Antoine de la Mothe Cadillac, on July 24, 1701, established the colony and town of Fort Pontchartrain du Detroit. From the date of its founding, Detroit was designed to be the commercial and administrative center of the interior of the continent. Always it has been the gathering place of Men of Affairs, Army officers, merchants, explorers, travelers and administrators. These men and their gifted women-folk have leavened the local Society with the best culture of France, England and America.

Although destined to become a great city, Detroit has endured its share of misfortunes. Twice it has experienced the horrors of an Indian siege in 1703 and 1712; it has surrendered to conquering armies; repeatedly, it has been the objective of hostile campaigns which failed of achieving their goal and five times its flag has changed. Three different nations have claimed its allegiance; repeatedly, it has been ravaged by epidemics, fires, and financial panics; and once was burned completely to the ground on June 11, 1805.

During Detroit's struggle for greatness, her many fires both tragic and spectacular, have been recorded by historians. Since the landing of Cadillac in 1701 and up to the arrival of our first workable fire engine "Protection No. 1" in 1825, all our fires were fought by bucket brigade. It was on February 17, 1827, when a fire broke out in the Abbott and Converse Brewery on the riverfront and spread to other buildings. Here our new fire engine was used for the first time.

During the first decade of our Volunteer Fire Department, bucket brigades were often used to augment the water supply of the early type hand engines. It was on December 13, 1835, at a Sunday morning fire at Brush and Larned that the bucket brigade was used for the last time in Detroit.

Between 1825 and 1860, our volunteer fire companies fought all of Detroit's fires. With major conflagrations occurring on April 27, 1837 and on January 1, 1842, which destroyed a large portion of business establishments south of Jefferson. Another hugh fire on May 9, 1848, in a warehouse at the foot of Bates St. owned by Joseph Campau burned out one quarter of the City and most of the business district. Twelve years later, on June 3, 1860, when a spectacular fire destroyed the D. M. Richardson Match Factory, this was the last fire in the City to be fought by the hand engine companies.

Subsequent to the establishment of our first paid steam fire engine company in October 1860, the first major fire was on March 7, 1863 when 50 buildings burned during a Civil Disturbance. Three steam fire companies and volunteers fought the fire for 9 hours. The next large blaze occurred on April 26, 1866 at the foot of Brush Street at the Detroit and Milwaukee R.R. yards. Several warehouses, a passenger train and the ferry boat, Windsor, burned with a loss of 22 lives. This was Detroit's first $1,000,000 fire. The following year on August 17, 1867, at the Gage fire on Woodward Avenue, John Miller of Engine 3 became the first paid fireman to lose his life.

It was on October 9, 1871 during the Great Chicago Fire that our City received an urgent call for assistance. Engine Companies 3 and 6 loaded their steam fire engines and hose reels aboard a special train and responded to aid the Chicago firefighters.

The most spectacular fire during the early years of our steam fire engine era was on April 29, 1875 when the huge Weber Furniture factory burned at Montcalm & John R. This nightime fire was so vivid the reflection was seen in Owosso. — Other tragic and spectacular fires continued to plague our city and here are some of the most notable:

Jan. 1, 1886 - D. M. Ferry Seed Co. Brush & Croghan (Monroe).

Jan. 27, 1893 - Capitol High School (former State Capitol) State & Griswold.

Nov. 23, 1893 - Edson & Moore Dry Goods Co. Bates & Jefferson, seven employees died when trapped on the upper floors. New fire boat & water tower used for the first time.

Oct. 5, 1894 - Keenan & Jahn Furniture Warehouse Woodward & Gd. River, five paid firemen and one volunteer lost their lives under a falling wall.

Nov. 6, 1895 - Detroit Journal Building Larned & Shelby, a boiler explosion & fire killed 37 civilians.

Oct. 7, 1897 - Detroit Opera House and surrounding area Campus Martius & Woodward.

Nov. 26, 1901 - Pemberthy Injector Co. Brooklyn & Abbott, thirty employees killed in an explosion.

Apr. 13, 1904 - Cadillac Automobile Co. Cass & York.

Jan. 8, 1907 - Michigan Stove Works Jefferson & Adair, one spectator killed when Ladder 10's horses bolted after an explosion occurred during the fire.

May 13, 1907 - Steamer City of Cleveland The Third Foot of Orleans, $550,000 loss.

Dec. 26, 1913 - Michigan Central Depot Foot of Third.

Apr. 27, 1915 - Belle Isle Bridge Jefferson & East Gd. Blvd., red hot coals falling from a tar wagon crossing the bridge ignited the wood flooring. Loss $100,000.

Feb. 2, 1917 - Saxon Motor Co. Meldrum & Benson, temperature was five below zero with a loss of $538,700.

Mar. 4, 1917 - Field's Suit & Cloak Co. Woodward & Gd. River, five firemen died when all five floors collapsed.

Aug. 1, 1919 - Wadsworth Mfg. Co. Jefferson & Connor's Creek, site of present Chrysler plant. Loss, $1,411,700.

Feb. 9, 1921 - Belle Isle Coliseum Jefferson & Field, loss was $109,600.

Jul. 22, 1925 - Gladstone Apartments Gladstone & Lawton, loss set at $206,100 blaze.

Jul. 4, 1926 - F. M. Sibley Lumber Co. Conner & E. Outer Drive. Due to lack of hydrant long relays were used, plant was a total loss in this $201,000 blaze.

Apr. 23, 1927 - Briggs Manufacturing Co. Russell & Harper, this was the City's first $2,000,000 fire with the loss of 22 lives when the paint department exploded.

Sep. 20, 1929 - Study Club Vernor & Woodward, twenty-two patrons burned to death or were suffocated attempting to escape the flames. The fire was put out with one hose line.

Mar. 15, 1930 - American Upholstering Co. West Jefferson, the fire loss in this fifth alarm was $223,300.

Apr. 28, 1930 - John F. Ivory Storage Co. West Jefferson & 10th, This building was a total loss in excess of $200,000.

Apr. 27, 1932 - Detroit Sulphite Pulp & Paper Co. West Jefferson & Anspatch, huge piles of cord-wood burned for six days. Both fire boats worked on this fire, The James Battle and the John Kendall.

Feb. 25, 1935 - Western High School Scotten & W. Vernor, loss was $200,000.

Oct. 28, 1936 - Currier Lumber Co. Van Dyke & E. Davison.

May 10, 1937 - Avance Glove Mfg. Co. West Jefferson & Griswold.

Mar. 10, 1938 - Goodwill Industries Beaubien & Mechanic St. A Detroit fireman on his way to Headquarters had the Gratiot street car on which he was riding stopped and pulled Box 54.

Apr. 3, 1942 - Michigan State Fair Buildings (Chevrolet exhibit area and others) Woodward & St. Fair.

Oct. 8, 1943 - David Stott Flower Mill (vacated) W. Warren & 17th.

Feb. 24, 1944 - Fisher Wall Paper Co. Randolph & E. Congress. The fire loss on this fifth alarm was $131,900.

Apr. 17, 1945 - Detroit Light Guard Armory East Larned & Randolph.

Aug. 13, 1945 - Export Box & Sealer Co. Grand River & 15th, an explosion and fire killed 21 employees. The fire loss on the building and contents was $325,000.

Feb. 14, 1948 - L. A. Young Spring & Wire Co. This factory building at 9200 Russell Street went to five alarms before being brought under control.

Jul. 27, 1948 - Rickel Malt Co. Adelaide & Rivard, the crew of Ladder 2 barely escaped with their lives when a roof penthouse exploded in a fire-ball.

Dec. 30, 1949 - Aurora Refining Co. South Dix & Oakwood.

Feb. 28, 1953 - Spitz Furniture Co. Baldwin & Gratiot. Within an hour this five story brick building was destroyed along with the adjoining former Engine House No. 20. Detroit's first 1936 Seagrave sedan pumper was destroyed by a falling wall while running as Engine 41.

Aug. 12, 1953 - General Motors Hydromatic Transmission on Plymouth Road in Livonia burned. This $54 million dollar fire was the nations largest industrial loss. Detroit along with several suburbs assisted Livonia firemen. The smoke pall could be seen in Mt. Clemens.

May 2, 1956 - Fred Sanders Store Woodward & Campus Martius, the fire loss on this fifth alarm was $667,500.

Jan. 17, 1959 - Tuller Hotel Park & Bagley. Starting in a ground floor retail store the fire spread throughout the lobby area with three employees burning to death in an elevator and 350 other guests escaped.

Feb. 9, 1959 - Packard Plant East Gd. Blvd & NYC Belt line R.R. Two separate four & five alarm fires in the same complex within the space of a few hours.

Mar. 2, 1961 - Higgins & Frank Clothing Store Washington Blvd. & Grand River.

Apr. 10, 1963 - Briggs Mfg. Co. (block long vacated factory) Meldrum & Benson, flames leaped across Benson Ave. and severely damaged Our Lady of Sorrows Church.

Aug. 4, 1964 - Ditzler Color Co. West Chicago & Roselawn.

May 21, 1965 - Statler-Hilton Hotel Washington Blvd. & Park.

June 19, 1966 - Former Mich. Central R.R. Depot (Vacant warehouse) Foot of Third St., Engine 8 lost their Seagrave pumper in a back-draft at this blaze.

June 20, 1966 - Lauri Bros. Warehouse East Larned & Leib, this was the second fifth alarm within a 24-hour period.

7/23-28, 1967 - Detroit experienced the worst civil disturbance in our nation's history. During the worst of the rioting there were 1,682 fires including 276 runs by mutual-aid fire departments from suburbs and Windsor. More than 5,000 citizens were burned out of their homes with a total loss estimate of $12,700,500 and 42 deaths were reported. The largest single business loss was the Famous Furniture & Upholstering Co. Jul. 23-24th at 3928-90 Gibson Ave set at $1,292,666.

Jul. 15, 1968 - Darby's Restaurant & others. West Seven Mile & Wyoming, $443,685 loss determined.

Jul. 23, 1968 - Industrial Public Warehouse Riopelle & Atwater, smoke from this fifth alarm plus fire was seen in Pt. Huron, loss was $305,000.

Apr. 15, 1970 - Danny's Gin Mill & The Dr. Golden Bldg. Shelby & State.

Jan. 1, 1971 - Hausman Steel Corp. 2450 Hubbard Ave., loss: $1,179,900.

Jan. 5, 1972 - Topinka's Country House Restaurant Seven Mile & Telegraph Rd., fire damage was $750,000.

Jul. 24, 1973 - Mid-West Paper Co. East Grand Blvd. & Mitchell. This $6,000,000 fire took several days to extinguish.

Jul. 24, 1973 - Follies Theatre Monroe & Cadillac Square.

Sep. 26, 1973 - Farr Moving & Storage Co. Alexandrine & Woodward. This fifth alarm loss was $1,500,000.

Mar. 28, 1975 - Usher Oil Co. 9010 Roselawn Ave. This fifth alarm required an additional 17 engines, five ladder and 1 squad company plus all the foam units in the city to bring under control.

In 1976, The City of Detroit faced with a severe budget crisis was forced to lay off 235 firefighters and close down eight engine and two ladder companies. The firefighters have since been returned to duty and new additional personnel are being trained in 1977 to reactivate some of the closed companies.

The year 1976, also saw an all-time high in the number of extra alarm fires. (132). There were: 76 seconds, 35 thirds, 14 fourth s and seven fifth alarms.

ALL FIFTH ALARMS IN 1976 ARE SHOWN
No. 1. Feb. 10, - Parkside Bowling Alley Lenox & E. Warren.
No. 2. Feb. 19, - Vacant factory, garage & two dwellings Algonquin & Kercheval.
No. 3. Mar. 22, - Bowl-O-Drome Bowling Alley Dexter & Waverly.
No. 4 Apr. 7, - Apartment building 79 West Alexanderine nr. Woodward.
No. 5. Jun. 1, - Owen School (vacated) Vermont & Myrtle.
No. 6. Jul. 4, - Warehouse Green & Erie.
No. 7. Oct. 13, - Kirlin Electric Co. Russell & Trombley.

July 25, 1977 - Quality Discount Furniture Co. & other commercial stores Seven Mile & Gratiot.

Note, up to the time this book went to press in September, 1977, this was the only fifth alarm of the year. Concurrent with laid-off fire fighters being returned to duty there has been a dramatic decrease of extra alarms in 1977. Detroit can be proud of its Fire Department, one of the finest in the nation.

The Board Of Fire Commissioners

1867 - 1974

The Legislature of the State of Michigan, in 1867, by Act Number 453, authorized the mayor of the City of Detroit to appoint a board of four Fire Commissioners, whose duty it would be to systematically organize the Detroit Fire Department. While the Commissioners themselves would serve without recompense, it was the beginning of the first paid Fire Department in Detroit.

Throughout the many years since the inception of the board, many titans in industry, commerce and finance have served the citizens of Detroit in the capacity of Fire Commissioner. With few exceptions, the commissioners served with honor and distinction. Detroit, through their collective efforts, has been fortunate to have one of the finest Fire Departments in the nation, and traditionally at a per capita cost that has consistently been among the lowest in the nation.

The Board of Fire Commissioners under the charters of the city have been responsible for the administration of the department. All promotions, appointments and personnel matters became the sole purvey of the board. The commission normally met once each week to conduct the policy meetings of the department. The commission's full time representative in the department was the secretary of the board, appointed by the board with approval of the mayor.

The members of the last Board of Fire Commissioners appointed by a mayor, ironically, lobbied collectively before the charter study commisson of the City of Detroit to recommend that the Board of Fire Commissioners be abolished in favor of a single paid commissioner. It came to pass then that on June 26, 1974, the Board of Fire Commissioners officially met for the last time, thus terminating over one hundred and seven years of continuous service to the City of Detroit.

. . . M. M. Hollen

The last Board of Fire Commissioners to serve the citizens of Detroit. Left to right, Melvin D. Jefferson, President; Anthony J. Szymanski, Commissioner; Ben B. Fenton, Commissioner and William S. Schindler, Vice-President. The original Fire Commission was created by the Michigan State Legislature to direct the affairs of the Detroit Fire Department and the first meeting of the new Commission was held on April 1, 1867. Wm. Duncan was elected President and T. H. Hinchman, L. H. Cobb and J. W. Sutton were members. B. Franklin Baker served as Secretary to the original Commission. This 1974 photograph was taken just prior to the new City Charter being adopted on July, 1. The new charter provided for a full time Commissioner and an Assistant Deputy Commissioner. Melvin D. Jefferson was appointed as the new Commissioner and Phillip F. Gorak, Deputy.

Detroit Fire Department - Original "Advisory Board of Fire Commissioners". Appointed December 2, 1974: (standing, left to right) Virgil Smith, Ben Fenton (deceased), Margaret Jones and John Gaylord. (seated) Commissioner, Melvin Jefferson and Deputy Commissioner, Phillip F. Gorak. The Board serves as a non-governing body appointed by the Mayor, and to advise the Mayor and the Fire Commissioner on matters relative to the Fire Department.

The Hundred Club

The Hundred Club of Detroit was founded in 1950 to help provide for the widows and dependents of policemen and firemen who lose their lives in the line of duty. The area covered is Wayne, Oakland and Macomb counties, and the Michigan state troopers throughout the state.

When a police officer or firefighter dies in the line of duty, a check is immediately delivered to the widow to relieve immediate cash problems, and shortly thereafter her debts and financial circumstances are considered by the disbursement committee and the necessary assistance given.

The Hundred Club also has a scholarship fund which is available to the children of police officers and fire fighters killed in the line of duty, and is available to high school graduates who want to go to college. The program includes state supported, community or private colleges; schools of nursing; and trade schools, such as secretarial, mechanics, electronics, computer operations, etc.

The Hundred Club of Detroit is a non-profit, charitable organization incorporated under the laws of the state of Michigan, and the benefits for the widows and children are paid from contributions of the members. There is a substantial amount of money in the treasury. The Hundred Club has no offices, no salaries, no politics and no endorsements, and does not want any publicity as to the work it does.

The Fire Mutual

Over the past 45 years, a group of men bonded together by their distinction as employees of the Detroit Fire Department, have collectively provided death and non-duty disability benefits to 1080 members, active and retired, of their organization.

This organization, formalized in title as the Detroit Fire Department Mutual Benefit Fund on January 1st, 1932, and known more simply today as the FIRE MUTUAL, has provided nearly three million dollars cash benefits to its' members or their beneficiaries.

Basically, we have today a group of Fire personnel that has grown in numbers over the past four decades, from 800 to todays 2100 regular and 1600 Active Mutual members.

Members whose very membership is dedicated to providing a basic and essential death benefit to it's body, at the lowest of cost; and in the instance of an off-duty disability, to provide a benefit where so little often exists.

On October 15, 1958, the Detroit Fire Department Active Men's Mutual was formed from the nucleus of the than existing Mutual membership. Essentially, those members who elected to join the Active Mutual, were providing for and hence protected by an increased benefit for either death while on the active roster of the Department, or for a off-duty disability that might occur while still an active member.

Certainly the economics of the time justified such an organization.

Today, some 45 years since its' formal appearance, the Fire Mutual, owing graditude to it's fire-fighters, the inspectors and arson investigators, members of central office, apparatus and training divisions, as well as the old telegraph employees of the public lighting commission, together have increased and protected all Mutual benefits payable through the future. Consequently, the Fire Mutual will continue to remain for todays member, and retirees of years past, a viable and effective organization providing a appreciable benefit to its' member in need.

Behind the scenes, accepting the responsibility for the dictates of its' by-laws and membership, the Fire Mutual Board of Trustees of the years past, has often met, (although not out of clandestine nature), in such places as now vacated Engine House #2, an off corner of old Fire Headquarters, the backroom of Engine 31, a kitchen area at Engine 42, even a sprinkler room of the W. Warren Training School. Yet, regardless of where they met, it is evident that the actions of these men were paramount to the success of todays' Mutual.

Although nine members through the years, have composed the body of the Mutual Board of Trustees, by its' structure, the responsibility for the complete daily operations of the Mutual has been singularly that of the appointed Secretary-Treasurer.

Therefore, it is in highest appreciation of years of dedication and endeavor, that we add to these pages the following names of those who have lived so much a part of this organization, and whose responsibility in action, has seen that every member and/or beneficiary had received the end purpose of this fund.

The following three men were the Founders of the Fire Mutual, drawing up the necessary papers and publishing their intent to the Fire Department:

LATTER DAYS OF 1931
NEWELL COLLINS - Secretary, Engine #2
EDWARD G. GOELLNER - telegraph headquarters
JOSEPH A. CREED - Engine #2
1932-1934 WALTER R. ROBERTS
1935-1939 JOHN C. HILL (died in office)
1939-1951 AMBER BURNS (died in office)
1951-1953 EDWARD TALBOT
1954-1955 GEORGE PETSCH (died in office)
1955-1956 CLEM FISCHER
1957-1961 RAYMOND SPENCER
1962-1970 CHESTER LOPATA
1971-1974 LEONARD ZEMBRUSKI
1975-   ROBERT C. McCARTHY
                    BOARD OF TRUSTEES'
                    FIRE MUTUAL

Police And Firemen Retirement System

The present Retirement System covering all Policemen and Firemen in the City of Detroit was established by City Charter in July of 1941. Since that time several amendments to the orginal benefit plan have been adopted by the voters of the City. In November of 1951, November of 1953, July of 1965, and January of 1969 benefit improvements were added to the original Retirement Plan.

A Board of Trustees is vested with the general administration, management and responsibility for the proper operation of the Retirement System. The Board of Trustees consists of eleven members as follows: three fire fighters who are elected by the Fire Department members of the system under such rules and regulations as may be established by the Fire Commissioner, and three police officers who are elected by the Police Department members of the System under such rules and regulations as may be established by the Chief of Police.

There are also five Ex-Officio members representing City Government. They are as follows: The Mayor or Finance Director, City Treasurer or Deputy Treasurer, President of the City Council or a member of the City Council so designated to serve on the Board,

the Chief of Police and the Fire Commissioner.

The Charter requires that the Board of Trustees must hold a public meeting at least once a month, but the present Board is meeting once a week due to the volume of business to be transacted.

The benefits provided by the System to its members include the following: Service Retirement Benefits for members who have 25 years or more of active service, Duty Disability Benefits for members who become physically disabled due to performance of their duties as police officers or fire fighters; Non-Duty Disability Benefits when the disability is not related to job performance. In addition, there are Death Benefits for Widows and Children under 18 years of age for deaths of spouses.

The funds to pay for the benefits provided by the Retirement System come from three sources: City contributions, member contributions and interest return on investments.

At the present time there is a total of 6,327 active members in the System. Also, 5,581 beneficiaries are collecting in excess of 4 million dollars in benefits monthly!

Veteran's Of Foreign War Post No. 1339

The Detroit Fire Department VFW Post 1339 was organized by a civilan named Otto Silver in the year of 1924. Post 1339 received their Charter on the 26th of March, 1925 with 67 members. Since then the number has increased. This year we have a total enrollment of 157 members of whom 32 have Lifetime Memberships. Through the years, four members from this Post have been elected to be District Commanders, and our Fire Department Dr. Machlon was the VFW's Department Surgeon for a number of years. After 57 years of continuous membership, we have two Comrades who are Charter Members. They are Samuel Litton and Joseph H. Smith.

PLAQUE:

After World War II, a bronze Plaque was donated by our VFW Post 1339 to the Detroit Fire Department which is located in the lobby of Fire Headquarters. On the Plaque are listed the names of our Comrades and all Department Firemen who either died or were missing in action during the Second World War.

HONOR GUARD:

Our Honor Guard is one of our greatest achievements. They have consistently and honorably participated at great personal cost, in every function they have been called upon to be involved in. During the years our Honor Guard uniforms have changed in style,

and color, now being a red uniform and beret with black boots. Our Honor Guard is involved in the Memorial Day services at Elmwood and Mt. Elliot cemetery, plus parades, funerals and other functions. They have won many awards for their percision marching and drills. To be a member of this team is really a great achievement, as they are always in the top of their class.

Our Post is involved in many functions, some of them being the training of the Fire Department Personnel at the National Home, visits to the Ann Arbor Burn Center, various hospitals and nursing homes with gifts for the patients. Time and energy was also devoted the following programs, such as: Voice of Democracy, Community activities, Environmental Programs, Flag Presentations, National Legislative Services (Veteran's benefits), National Security and Foreign affairs and consulting with out Veterans on informing and assisting them to receive their earned Veteran's benefits.

POPPIES:

Each year our Members have actively participated in selling poppies made by their disabled Comrades in the Veteran's Hospital in order to help the patients with rehabilitation and financial aid. So please remember them next year — Be generous and buy a poppy. Help those who have given so much to us and our Country.

American Legion Post No. 75

The Detroit Fire Department American Legion Post #75 was founded in January of 1949 and carries the name of Arthur R. Peltier, a member of the Detroit Fire Department and one of the first to give his life in the service of our country in World War II.

The Post is active in the principles of the American Legion. In the past we have sponsored children to the Grace Bentley Summer Camp for Crippled Children, children to the Shrine Circus, and Christmas parties at the Christ Child Home. We also present Americanism Awards to 7th and 8th grade boys and girls, donate flags to Scout Troops, and help finance the Hospital Liaison Committee at the Veterans Hospital in Dearborn.

Our Color Guard participates in the Memorial Day Services with the Fire Department and at the Field Day ceremony.

The satisfaction of working on these worthwhile projects and the good fellowship with the post members are the reasons we are proud to be recognized as members of the Detroit Fire Department, Arthur R. Peltier, American Legion Post #75.

The Phoenix Of The Detroit Fire Department

The Phoenix is a community service organization comprised of black fire department employees. The name Phoenix is derived from Egyptian mythology; according to legend, the Phoenix, a beautiful, lone bird that lived in the Arabian Desert for 500 years, consumed itself in fire and rose renewed from its ashes to start another long life "WE AROSE FROM THE ASHES OF '67" is the motto of the new Phoenix. The organization was formed after the 1967 civil disturbance in Detroit. That disturbance has been the largest holocaust, to date, in the U.S. After that terrible time when many lives and great amounts of property were lost due to fire, it became apparent that the black fire fighters need to initiate positive programs of action designed to prevent a similar tragedy. To this end, the Phoenix programs are geared to:

1. Encourge citizen participation to promote good government
2. Inspire respect for the law
3. Generate action activities that will aid and encourage the wholesome development of Metropolitan Detroit youth
4. Bring about a mutual respect between Fire Department personnel and the total community

A two pronged methodology is used in pursuing the above objectives; active community involvement and institutional changes within the Detroit Fire Department.

The following are specific programs that the Phoenix are involved in:

I. SCHOOLS AND YOUTH PROGRAMS
   a. Members of the Phoenix acted in a Fire Safety skit entitled "King of the Fall Season". The skit was performed in Detroit elementary schools before over 30,000 students. The skit was taped by the Detroit Board of Education's TV station and aired over WTVS-TV 56.
   b. Members of the Phoenix participated in "Career Day Programs" in public schools promoting the fire service as a worthy career as part of a long range minority recruitment program.
   c. In cooperation with the Neighborhood Youth Corp (NYC) and the Catholic Youth Organization (CYO), members of the Phoenix taught fire fighting to 200 young men at the Fire Training Academy. The youth who were trained were named "Junior Phoenix Fire Cadets"
   d. Assisted the Detroit Police Department in setting up a Junior Police Department Cadet program similar to the Fire Department Cadet program.

II. CONTRIBUTIONS AND ASSISTANCE TO COMMUNITY ORGANIZATIONS
   a. Donated $1,000.00 to the Sickle Cell Anemia Drive of 1972.
   b. Secured and delivered food and toys to burned out families through the Michigan Shelter during the Christmas seasons of 1970, 1971 and 1972.
   c. Donated $150.00 to the Detroit Chapter of the Wilberforce Alumni.
   d. Set up and manned fire service information booths at the Afro-American Ethnic Festival and the Michigan State Fair.

III. SPORTS
   a. Established a Phoenix bowling league for youngsters 11 to 14 years.
   b. Held annual kite flying contests for children under 12.
   c. Established a Phoenix basketball team for teams. They participated in the Detroit Northwestern Basketball League.
   d. Assisted the Optimist Club of Central Detroit with their annual track meets.

IV. WORKED ON COMMITTEES TO BRING OUT THE FOLLOWING
   a. Assisted in revamping the Civil Service Test for Fire Fighters in 1970.
   b. Assisted in the minority recruitment program
   c. Studied the height and weight requirements for Fire Fighters and recommended changes.

Detroit Fire Department Band

The Detroit Fire Department Band was organized on April 17, 1920. The idea that this Department should have a band that was truly representative of the personnel of the Department, was born in the minds of three men. Captain Anthony Delesie, Glenn Middleditch and Otto Klatt, then members of Rescue No. 1. Captain Delesie wrote the Fire Commission for permission to organize the band, which was immediately granted. The task was really a great one as the number of men in the department that had musical talent was small and men were induced to purchase an instrument and study it. That they had succeeded is beyond question.

In 1926, with a membership of 44 men, the band gave radio concerts for three years on station WJR, which was highly appreciated, as thousands of letters from radio fans all over over the country will attest.

One of the many honors the band received was in 1926 when it was selected by the City to escort Lt. Commander John Phillip Sousa from the M.C.R.R. depot to Orchestra Hall. Commander Sousa highly praised the band on its fine appearance and playing ability.

It is not known who directed the band until 1946 when Walter Handlik became the first civilian to direct the band. He directed the band until his death in 1958. Incidently, his son James Handlik is presently a Lieutenant on the Fire Department.

The band was then placed under the directorship of retired FEO Leonard Shawpeter until 1961.

The band then looked to the Windsor Fire Dept. and Capt. Phillip Murphy was given the job of directing the band.

Because of ill health Mr. Murphy retired from directing the band and passed the directorship on to Captain Alex Meldrum of the Fire Department and is presently still directing the band.

The Chief of Department appoints a band manager to be responsible for all band affairs. Some of the men who held this job thru the years have been Chief Erickson, Chief Edmund DeCaussin, Chief Paul Karabes, Chief Raymond Hoffman, Chief Frank Van Turnout, Chief Robert Engel, and its present manager Chief Edward Tujaka.

The band plays at civic affairs, parades, memorial day services, gives concerts during fire prevention week, plays at all field days, and the sad duty of playing at funerals of members who die in the line of duty. Also members of the band have volunteered their time since 1963 to assist the Police Dept. band for policemen's funerals. They also play concerts, at veterans hospital, and old folks homes.

In 1958 under the leadership of Robert Engel, a combo was formed to play for dancing at mixed retirement parties. Until his retirement in 1974 Bob Engel and his Five Alarms played for over 150 retirement parties.

The combo is still playing although down to three men from this department and an accordian player who is a fireman in the Warren Fire Department.

In 1964 a German Band was formed under the leadership of FEO Andrew Custage, which played at stag retirement parties and civic affairs which warranted a small group.

In 1964 Lt. Joseph Krolik took over the leadership and also changed the group's name to the Redshirt Band. It still plays at civic affairs, stag retirement parties and plays under the stands at our field day.

Our Fire Department Clown Team

The Detroit Fire Department Clown Team has been in existence officially for over thirty years. Before this there is little written record. Although there were clowns prior to World War II, during the war years there was no organized clown teams.

In February of 1946, after serving his country Larry Scarpace joined the Detroit Fire Department. Upon learning that Scarpace had done shows with Bob Hope and other entertainers as a part of the USO tours he was persuaded to perform in the Field Day that summer with his own one man act. Because of his success in the Field Day of '46, Scarpace was inspired to organize an eight man clown team for the following year. This was to be the official start of the Clown Team as it is known today.

The DFD Clown Team is well known throughout the Detroit area. The work they do is often unheralded. Their appearance at children's hospitals, nursing homes, etc. receives very little publicity, but they are there to entertain and cheer the young and the young at heart when they most need cheering. They have participated in many functions as part of their efforts to raise thousands of dollars for the Burn Center and other charitable organizations. Their acts and antics are always a high point of the Annual Field Day. They originate their own acts and costumes, build their own props for the various skits and donate their time solely for the entertainment of others. Their reward is your applause and laughter.

Hockey Team

1960 to 1976

The Detroit Fire Department hockey team was organized in the year 1960 through the efforts of Ed. Wardle, Gene Barterian and Bud Brown, with the sanction of Chief of Department, Lawrence Daly. The team was then entered in the Detroit Industrial Hockey League.

In its infancy the team, with make-shift uniforms, wasn't much to look at in appearance, but through sheer intestinal fortitude, and a little luck, ended it's premier season with an admirable record of 6 wins, 3 losses and 1 tie. As our team embarked on its third season there was a tremendous change in appearance and play of the team. Through the generosity of Mr. Ivan Ludington Sr., owner of the Ludington News, and former Fire Commissioner, Fred Harris Sr., now deceased, the hockey team purchased their first uniforms, royal blue, trimmed in red and white. Also in the 1963 season, the team was blessed with several young players who decided to make the Detroit Fire Department their career. Sporting this new look the team launched its season by destroying teams like Edison 12-2, Chrysler 9-2 and the Gas Co. 9-3, in league play. Then to climax the season our team beat the defending champs, Michigan Bell Telephone Co. 3-2 to win the playoffs and their first championship.

Challenges started to come in from the Windsor, Ontario fire fighters, Chicago Fire Department and our own Detroit Police Department. The Detroit Fire Fighters Association, local 344, combined with the hockey club, and met these challenges with a series of benefit games, to be played once a year, to raise money for local charities. These games, a total of seven in all, raised $54,000 for such organizations as the Goodfellows of Detroit, the Michigan Burn Center, in Ann Arbor, and the Salvation Army to purchase a new canteen truck to serve the Detroit and suburban fire fighters at all multiple alarm fires.

The first benefit game was staged at the Cobo Arena, with the Detroit Police Department as opponents. Before a crowd of nearly 10,000, cheering fans, D.F.D. team defeated the Detroit Police Team, to the tune of 12-2. Jim Siebert, once labeled, the top amateur hockey player in Michigan, skated away with the most valuable player award by scoring 3 goals and assisting four others. Several representatives of the Chicago Fire Department witnessed this awesome display of power but still issued a challenge to the D.F.D. team for the 1964 seson. Local 344, Detroit Fire Fighters Assn., chartered a bus for the trip to Chicago. Chicago's fire fighters rolled out the red carpet in the true spirit of comradeship so characteristic of the Windy City. The game itself was reminiscent of play between two National Hockey League teams of this era. The Chicago hockey team had tasted defeat only once in three years in the Chicago City league.

The immovable object (Chicago) played valiantly but they were no match for the irresistible force (Detroit) as they fell to defeat 11-6. The next three seasons the Detroit Fire Dept. continued to reign supreme in the Industrial League winning 34 games and only losing 3, also gaining 4 straight championships; a record that hasn't been matched to this date. During the 1966-67 season the D.F.D. started to know the bitter taste of defeat. The team was going through a period of transition. Several veteran players had hung up their skates and the new replacements couldn't fill the void. The team, like true champions, took their defeats with the same grace they displayed as winners.

With a determined effort the 1967-68 team had produced their 5th championship in 8 years; but couldn't carry the baton any farther until the 1973-74 season. Here, after a long drought, won their 6th. and last championship as the Detroit Industrial League folded two years later. The 16 year record of the D.F.D. hockey team was 122 wins, 60 losses and 20 ties and the record for benefit games stands at 6 wins, 1 loss.

Detroit Firemen's Fund Association

The Detroit Firemen's Fund Assoiation was organized as a non-profit organization on March 16, 1866 and was incorporated on April 13, 1867. The Fund was formed to assist the widows and orphans of Firefighters and to assist Firefighters who have become disabled. The Fund has also purchased and maintains burial plots for Firefighters who express the desire to be interred in close proximity to their firefighting brothers. Each year on Memorial Day, services are held at the cemetery to honor our fallen brothers. The services include a uniformed parade of firefighters, the Department Band, and the Honor Guard of both the V.F.W. and the American Legion. Wreaths are placed and Taps are sounded in an impressive ceremony which in '77 was attended by over 100 firefighters who wished to pay homage.

In order to finance these various services, dues are collected from all members. A Yearbook is issued each year through the donations of local merchants and friends of the Department, and a Field Day is held at Tiger Stadium, the home of the Detroit Tigers. The 55th Annual Field Day for 1977, was held on August 21st. The Field Day is financed through the support of the citizens of Detroit and its' environs. This is primarily a display by the Fire Department Thrill Team with demonstrations showing rope slides, the use of the life net, ladder raising and varied other feats. We also have a Clown Team composed entirely of firefighters who perform with expertize at this event. The Clown Team also donates their time year round, to amuse and entertain children in hospitals and orphanages. They give freely of their time in rest homes and nursing homes to alleviate the boredom of our senior citizens. We engage a limited number of professional acts, in '76 we had high wire acts, in previous years we have had the "Human Cannonball" and this year we engaged "Superman", Guy Gibby, who performs feats of strength which includes pulling a car with his teeth. Each year one member of the Department is chosen to receive the "Jefferson Medal of Valor" for what is deemed to be the most heroic act of the year. This presentation was made at the Field Day. The '77 award went to Firefighter Edward Smith III, who is following in the footsteps of his father who is a present battalion chief in the Department.

The Firemen's Fund is composed of nine elected Trustees who serve a three year term, plus an ex-officio member, the Chief of Department. It is the duty of the Trustees to handle the funds of this organization in accordance with the By-Laws, which regulates all financial transactions.

Frederick H. Nicholls
President, Detroit Firemen's Fund

Another "First" for the Detroit Fire Department. Delivered in October, 1977 and with a pump capacity of 1,500 gallons per minute, this huge Seagrave is the largest pumper ever to be delivered to the city. Assigned to Engine 9, this was the first Seagrave pumper to be purchased by the department since November, 1967. The new unit will provide ample pressure to serve the new Renaissance Center. Other features are a new low-profile design, improved cab visibility, wider jump seats and an adjustable steering column.

This scene taken on Tuesday, July 25, 1967 at the Command Post at Engine 52, Manistique & E. Warren was the third day of Detroit's Civil Disturbance. An engine and ladder company would respond to any fire on the east side of the city from this location. National Guardsmen or state troopers responded to each fire, 2 on a pumper and three on a ladder company. A similar command post was established at W. Warren & Lawton Ave. at the Training Academy to handle all the west side runs.

This action photo taken by Barney Wasowicz was at the fifth alarm Cenco Medical Supply Co. fire at Woodward & E. Canfield Ave. on July 31, 1975. Shown in the foreground is the 1974 Ward LaFrance pumper of Engine 17 (Second & Burroughs). The monitor nozzle mounted on top of the $45,500 pumper was being used to help control the blaze.

One of Detroit's several fires involving double-bottom gasoline tanker trucks. After a rash of nine such accidents in Wayne, Oakland and Macomb Counties in which 15 persons were injured and three deaths occurred in 1977 the Governor of Michigan ordered a ban on the use of the "Pup" trailers in all metropolitan areas between 6 a.m. & 10 p.m.

A rare unpublished photo of Detroit's first Seagrave sedan pumper in action. The fire was at the Advance Glove Manufacturing Company on West Jefferson & Griswold, May 10, 1937. This same apparatus, while running as Engine 41 was demolished by a falling wall at the Spitz Furniture Store fire on Feb. 28, 1953 at Baldwin & Gratiot.

Mankind's battle against fire in one form or another has been going on as long as civilization itself.

During the next hour there is a statistical likelihood that more than 300 fires will rage somewhere in this nation:

- Killing 1 person
- Injuring 34 people
- Destroying $300,000 worth of property

On an annual basis:

- Fire kills 12,000 people
- Fire injures 300,000 people
- Fire destroys 11 Billion dollars worth of property

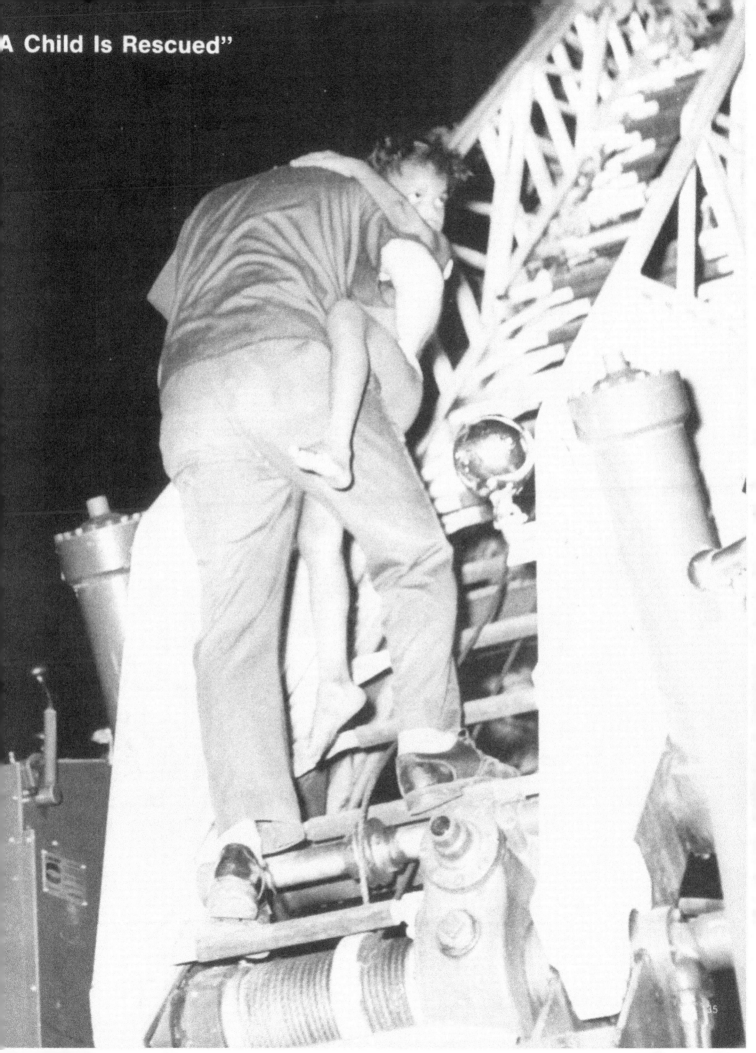

"A WEST SIDE WORKER ON A COLD DAY"

This 1940 photo of one of the first D.F.D. clown teams featured Pop-eye The Sailor of the Windsor Fire Department (shown under the car). The fun-makers were promoting the 18th Annual Field Day at the time.

Detroit fire fighters battled 20-foot high flames and three separate explosions at this east side fifth-alarm-plus blaze at the Mid-West Paper Products Co., 2250 East Grand Boulevard near Chene St. Thirty-two pieces of equipment including the snorkel were used to battle the fire which broke out at 11:57 p.m. on July 24, 1973. This was the largest fire to be seen in Detroit since 1970 and there was only one minor injury. A second team of 135 fire fighters were called in at 5:30 a.m. because of heat exhaustion of the original responding crews. It was several days before the fire was completely extinguished in the countless bales of paper.

Five fire fighters and five persons on a southbound Woodward streetcar were injured on November 28, 1950 when the car crashed into Ladder 1 at Woodward & Fort Street. The fire company was responding to a small restaurant fire on Cadillac Square. The truck had entered the intersection just as the traffic light was changing from green to red, it had been raining and the motorman of the trolley car said he was unable to stop in time to avoid the collision. Injured in the mishap were Capt. John Wachowski, Richard Vettest, Daniel Deleggato, Lawrence Miles and Richard Van Raemdonck. The 1937 Seagrave was the first 100 ft. all-steel aerial ladder in the Detroit Fire Department and had a fully enclosed five-man cab. The unit was sent back to the Seagrave factory and rebuilt with a new tractor. The rig was returned to service on September 29, 1951 as Dept. 819 and re-assigned to Ladder 3. In 1969 it became an extra truck and was retired from the department in 1976.

DETROIT'S FIRE COMPANIES
AND
EMERGENCY MEDICAL UNITS

Over the years a number of Detroit fire stations have been relocated, or deactivated due to: close proximity of stations; shift of population and manufacturing areas; budgetary problems; freeway construction and urban renewal programs.

The following list of engine and ladder companies indicates their location when they went out of service as well as the companies still active in 1977.

ENGINE COMPANIES

Company organized		No.	Location	Month & year company went out of service	
Oct.	1860	1	Larned & Washington Blvd.	Jan. 1975 /back in ser. 1/78	
Jan.	1861	2	St. Antoine N. of Larned	May	1940
Jul.	1861	3	Montcalm, west of Park	Mar.	1976
Feb.	1865	4	Eighteenth, N. of Lafayette	Mar.	1976
Jun.	1865	5	Alexandrine, west of Cass		
Apr.	1868	6	Russell & Wilkins		
Feb.	1874	7	Lafayette & Mt. Elliott	Apr. 1976 /back in ser. 1/78	
Nov.	1873	8	Bagley & Sixth		
Apr.	1880	9	Lafayette, W. of St. Antoine		
Jul.	1883	10	Vinewood & West Grand Blvd.		
Jan.	1884	11	Gratiot & Grandy	Jan.	1975
			(now F.D. Museum)		
Dec.	1886	12	Warren & Lawton	Mar.	1976
Jan.	1887	13	Milwaukee & Riopelle	Mar.	1976
Feb.	1888	14	Vinewood & West Grand Blvd.	May	1940
Dec.	1888	15	Hubbard, north of Fort	May	1940
Jul.	1893	16	Fire Boat, Foot of 24th	Apr.	1976

Engine 16 will return to service when new fire boat is delivered

Jun.	1893	17	Second & Burroughs		
May	1893	18	Mt. Elliott & Sylvester		
Jan.	1894	19	Elmwood & Fort	Jun.	1949
Jul.	1896	20	Gratiot & Baldwin	May	1940

Engine 20 was reactivated Jun. 1961 at Detroit City Airport as a crash and foam unit, Conner & Gratiot

Jul.	1896	21	Linwood, north of Calvert		
Jul.	1896	22	Michigan, east of Military		
Jul.	1899	23	East Grand Boulevard & Moran		
Jul.	1899	24	Kenilworth, E. of Woodward	May	1940
Jun.	1901	25	Fire Boat, Foot of Mc Dougall	May	1940
Jun.	1901	26	Crane & Brinket		
Nov.	1902	27	Junction & Rogers		
May	1905	28	Milwaukee & Riopelle	Ma y	1940
May	1907	29	West Jefferson & Solvay		
May	1907	30	Rivard & Livingston	May	1940

Engine 30 was reactivated in May 1951 at Meyers & Florence

Jan.	1909	31	West Grand Boulevard & Cobb Pl.		
Jan.	1909	32	Jefferson & Hart		
May	1912	33	Lafayette & Lawndale		
Nov.	1910	34	Livernois, south of Walton		
Dec.	1911	35	Kenilworth, E. of Woodward		

Jan.	1913	36	Miller & Helen		
Nov.	1916	37	Central & Dix	Apr. 1976 /back in ser. 1/78	
Jun.	1915	38	Coplin, north of Jefferson		
Jul.	1916	39	Taylor & Byron		
Jul.	1916	40	Twelfth & La Belle		
Oct.	1916	41	Rohns & Warren		
Feb.	1917	42	West Chicago, west of Livernois		
Jul.	1921	43	Davison & Goddard		
Sep.	1921	44	Seven Mile & John R.	Apr. 1976 /back in ser. 1/78	
Jan.	1922	45	St. Jean, north of Mack		
Aug.	1921	46	Knodell & Grace		
Jul.	1922	47	Mt. Elliott & Davison		
Nov.	1924	48	Bayside & Sanders		
Nov.	1924	49	Grand River & Manor		
Mar.	1925	50	Houston-Whitter & Gratiot		
Jul.	1926	51	Livernois & Curtis		
Jul.	1926	52	Manistique, north of Warren		
Sept.	1926	53	Greenfield & Fenkell		
Jan.	1926	54	Grand River & Trinity		
Jul.	1927	55	Joy Road & Ashton		
Jul.	1927	56	Ryan & Hildale		
Sep.	1927	57	Burt Rd., N. of Schoolcraft		
Dec.	1928	58	Whittier & Lakepointe		
Aug.	1930	59	Curtis & Fenmore		
Jul.	1931	60	Hoover & Manning		

- LADDER COMPANIES -

Month & year company went out of service	Company organized		No.	Location		
Apr.	1965		Snorkel - Lafayette, w. of St. Antoine			
May	1864	1	Larned & Washington Blvd.	Oct. 1958 /back in ser. 1/64		
Aug.	1871	2	Larned, E. of St. Antoine	Nov.	1951	
Feb.	1881	3	Montcalm, west of Park			
Sep.	1884	4	Vinewood & West Gd. Blvd.	Apr. 1976 /back in ser. 1/78		
Jan.	1889	5	Russell & Wilkins	Mar.	1976	

eb.	1889	6	Lafayette & Mt. Elliott
Jun.	1893	7	Second & Burroughs
Jun.	1893	8	Junction & Rogers
Jan.	1894	9	Warren & Lawton
May	1898	10	Mt. Elliott & Sylvester
Jan.	1906	11	Milwaukee & Riopelle
Jan.	1908	12	Lafayette, west of Tenth
Jan.	1909	13	Lafayette & Lawndale
Nov.	1912	14	Crane & Brinket
Jan.	1911	15	Kenilworth, E. of Woodward
Dec.	1919	16	Miller & Helen
Dec.	1920	17	Twelfth & La Belle
Sep.	1921	18	Seven Mile & John R.
Sep.	1921	19	Shoemaker & French Road
May	1921	20	Alexandrine, west of Cass
Dec.	1921	21	West Chicago, west of Livernois
Mar.	1922	22	Mc Graw & Martin
Mar.	1923	23	Houston-Whittier & Gratiot
Jul.	1926	24	Livernois & Curtis
Sep.	1926	25	Greenfield & Fenkell
Jul.	1926	26	Grand River & Trinity
Jan.	1928	27	Joy Road & Ashton
Jul.	1927	28	Linwood, north of Calvert
Dec.	1927	29	Coplin, north of Jefferson
Sep.	1928	30	Mt. Elliott & Davison
Aug.	1942	31	Manistique, north of Warren

- TACTICAL MOBILE SQUAD COMPANIES -

Company organized		No.	Location	Month & year company went out of service
Oct.	1908	1	Larned & Washington Blvd.	Jan. 1978
Oct.	1910	2	Alexandrine, west of Cass	
Oct.	1912	3	East Grand Boulevard & Moran	
Jan.	1915	4	West Grand Boulevard & Cobb Pl.	
May	1947	5	Twelfth & La Belle	
Jul.	1951	6	Houston-Whitter & Gratiot	
Oct.	1951	7	Greenfield & Fenkell	
Mar.	1972	8	Central & Dix	Jan. 1978
Jan.	1972	9	Jefferson & Hart	Jan. 1978

** No. of tab cmds. 0064

*** Next highest mult. 0070

- BATTALION CHIEFS -

1 Lafayette, W. of St. Antoine
2 Joy Road & Ashton
3 Miller & Helen
4 Second & Burroughs
5 West Grand Boulevard & Cobb Pl.
6 Jefferson & Hart
7 Junction & Rogers
8 Seven Mile & John R.
9 Linwood, north of Calvert
10 Houston-Whittier & Gratiot
11 Curtis & Fenmore

12 Houston-Whittier & Gratiot (Out of ser. Jun. 1961)

- SPECIAL UNITS -

Department Ambulance & Medical Unit - Larned & Wash. Blvd.
Boat Tender No. 1 - Larned & Washington Blvd.

- STAND-BY RESERVE UNITS -

Floodlight Unit	Bagley & Sixth	(Eng. 8)
Foam Truck No. 1	Second & Burroughs	(Eng. 17)
Foam Truck No. 2	Russell & Wilkins	(Eng. 6)
Foam Truck No. 3	Lafayette & Mt. Elliott	(Lad. 6)
Hose Wagon No. 1	Russell & Wilkins	(Eng. 6)

Fire Headquarters	Larned & Washington Blvd.
Training Academy	West Warren & Lawton
Apparatus Bureau	Russell & Erskine
Communications	Chrysler Ser. Dr. & Macomb
E. M. S.	Merrill Plaisance & Third

*** No. of tab cmds. 0020
*** Next highest mult. 00

DETROIT FIRE DEPARTMENT

EMERGENCY MEDICAL UNITS

Unit organized		Medic No.	Location	Shares quarters with	
	1972	1	Taylor & Byron	Engine	39
Jun.	1972	2	West Chicago, west of Livernois	Engine	42
Jun.	1972	3	Meyers & Florence	Engine	30
Jun.	1972	4	Grand River & Trinity	Engine	54
Jun.	1972	5	Joy Road & Ashton	Engine	55
Jul.	1972	6	Alexandrine, west of Cass	Engine	5
Sep.	1972	7	Warren & Lawton	Ladder	9
Sep.	1972	8	Bagley & Sixth	Engine	8
Jul.	1972	9	West Jefferson & Solvay	Engine	29
Jul.	1972	10	Michigan, east of Military	Engine	22
Sep.	1972	11	Grandy & Gratiot (Out of ser. 3, 77)	Eng.	11
Dec.	1972	12	Jefferson & Hart	Engine	32
Dec.	1972	13	Milwaukee & Riopelle	Ladder	11
Jan.	1973	14	Rohns & Warren	Engine	41
Jan.	1973	15	Whittier & Lakepointe	Engine	58
Oct.	1972	16	Ryan & Hildale	Engine	56
Jul.	1975	17	Lafayette & Mt. Elliott	Ladder	6
Jul.	1975	18	Merrill Plaisance & Third in Palmer Park		

*** No. of tab cmds. 0126
*** Next highest mult. 0070

C. C. Woodard
D.F.D. Historian

Retirees Appreciation Fund

Raymond Vallad served in the Detroit Fire Department from February 19, 1917, to December 30, 1958, almost forty-one years, starting in 1917 at Engine 32 (Hart and Jefferson), in a two-rig, horse-drawn company, which comprised a small portion of the city's mostly horse-drawn steam apparatus in those days. Raymond Vallad advanced upward from a substitute pipeman to Cadet, to Fire Fighter and through the ranks to the top position of Chief of Department, retiring soon after at the age of 61 years nine months.

After ten years of retirement, but still keeping in close touch with the Department, his activities took him to a Department Officers Club Meeting on October 8, 1968, at the Belle Isle Casino. Seated at the same table were several other retired officers. The conversation got around to discussing ways by which retirees could assist the Detroit Fire Fighters Association, which had just negotiated a substantial salary increase for active membership, which means that the retired members would receive a generous increase in their pension checks. One of the officers remarked quite enthusiastically, "I wish we could do something to show our appreciation to the Union". That's where Chief Vallad spoke up. Holding out his hand toward his friends, he said, "O.K., give me your money and I will see to it that the Union gets it with your good wishes." There were some 30 or 35 dollars collected and turned over to George Younan, (then an officer in the union) in the name of the "D.F.D. RETIREES APPRECIATION FUND" as a show of appreciation for the increase in pension benefits.

Within the next months or so, Vallad had formulated and sent out a letter to all retirees throughout the U.S. and Canada explaining the purpose of the fund. At the same time, a telephone contact system was started and all retirees in the Detroit area were called. Retiree Ray Tanner did most of the calling over a three month period.

Soon contributions began arriving from the retirees with letters expressing their appreciation to the Union for getting the increase. Since then, Chief Vallad has received thousands of letters and contributions, personal request and problems from those living away from the City.

During the past nine years of its existance the Fund has enabled Chief Vallad to turn over approximately $55,000 to Local 344 as the retired men continue to express their gratitude to the Union.

The continued correspondence with the retired men keep Chief Vallad busy enough to dispel all forms of boredom during his retirement.

Officers Club

Our club, strictly a social club, was organized forty-four years ago on October 1, 1933. The first meetings were held at the old Fort Shelby Hotel and meals were served in the hotel dining room at very reasonable cost. A few years later, the club moved its meetings to the Public Lighting Building at the foot of Randolph Street. At that time, the good old fire barn cooks prepared the meals. Among them were guys like Oscar Hammerle and Vince Kracht, both long retired now but still members in good standing in our club.

Our first elected officers were:

Pres.—Chief Edward Rumsey, also Chief of Apparatus

Vice Pres.—Chief Wm. Rein, also Sec. to the Commission

Sec.-Treas.—Chief Louis Brunell

Sgt. at Arms—Capt. Joseph Appel

Remaining Board Members.

Chief Wm. Monson   Capt. John Weisgerber
Chief Herman Fleischer   Lieut. Danial Jordan
Lieut. Wm. Dacey

We have had twenty-nine presidents over the forty-four years.

All officers, active and retired, are members and we still enjoy lively meetings monthly from September through May every year. Meetings are held yearly from the east to west side of the city and the opposite units each month. Differing from years past, all retired members of the department are welcomed as guests and any active officer may bring guests from the active rolls of the department. The club has continued to flourish and there is great rivalry between retirees and active members attending these monthy meetings. Once each year we invite our Box 12, Box 42 and other fire buffs to join our festivities. It is always a very special night for everyone.

The present board pictured in this historical record

Pres.—Capt. Donald Donati

Vice Pres.—Chief John Fusting

Sec.—Capt. Donald LeBeau

Treas.—Lieut. Paul Langlois

Chrman.—Chief Ludwig Rupprecht

Chief Frank Szopko   Lieut. Andrew Kolar
Capt. Jay Smith   Capt. Alphonse Green
Lieut. Melvin Leskie

We no longer have the lively piano and song fests but the card games are very alive. The old fire stories will live on forever at these very enjoyable meetings. COME JOIN US.

Fire Fighters Association

THE DETROIT FIRE FIGHTERS ASSOCIATION

Although professional fire fighters had been organized locally and affiliated with the international association of fire fighters nationally, it was not until the early nineteen thirties that unionism took hold in the Detroit Fire Department.

With the advent of the Roosevelt Administration in 1932 and the Enactment of the Wagner Act, union efforts and organizing took a giant step forward, particularly in the automotive and allied industries here in Detroit. This new union fervor pervaded the minds and hearts of Detroit's Fire Fighters.

The path to actually forming the "Detroit Fire Fighters Association" was, to say the least, an extremely hard and rocky one. The administration of the department exercised most every device at their disposal to discourage and defeat this new adventure, including threatened lay-offs, threatened dismissals and many other reprisals too numerous to mention here. Organizing efforts were conducted in secret and meetings were held in some of the most unlikely places. However the spirit that gave birth to the idea itself was strong and viable. The organizing efforts prevailed and in May, 1933 the Detroit Fire Fighters Association was chartered as Local 344, of the International Association of Fire Fighters.

It was not to pass until many years later that public employees were actually, by law, given the right to organize. Thus the early beginnings of the Young Local were anything but smooth. The organization, from its inception until the early nineteen sixties, was legally a "De Facto Entity", recognized and finally accepted, but legally not a union. This "De Facto" label in no way deterred the very able and zealous leadership of the association from launching into a vigorous and formidable program of upgrading the plight of its members.

The preamble of its first constitution clearly stated its aims and goals.

"The purpose of this association and its publication, the Fire Fighter, is to promote and stimulate a true fraternal spirit among its members; the elevation and improvment of the moral, intellectual, social and economic conditions of its members; to foster a higher degree of skill and efficiency in the performance of departmental duties; the maintenance of proper remuneration for duties performed; the protection of the joint and individual rights of its members in the pursuit of their vocations; to unite the members of the Detroit Fire Department into one group whereby through our combined efforts we may protect ourselves against injustice and unjust discrimination."

The association throughout its forty-four years of existence has admirably adhered to its aforestated pledge. The early success of the union was enhanced considerably by its affiliation with county, state and national labor organizations which time and again lent their collective "clout" to aid the fire fighters. Prior to the enactment by law of the collective bargaining rights for fire fighters, much of the progress had to be achieved through referendum of the people involving much hard work and expenditure. In many other instances the association had to resort to the courts for redress. It should be noted that the union has always had the good foresight to retain capable and knowledgeable legal counsel. The membership likewise has, with few exceptions, always elected energetic and vibrant leaders to represent them. These combinations produced the chemistry to build the excellent record of achievement in keeping with the association's aims and purpose.

Today the Detroit Fire Fighters Association stands as a model of what united, collective effort can accomplish. The Detroit Fire Fighters are among the highest paid in the nation and their fringe benefits rate with the very best in any fire department. The union has lent its prestige and might to raising the standards of performance by its members in the pursuit of their duties, remaining ever vigilant to degradation and ever willing to assist in the process of improvement and progress.

The men of today's Fire Department indeed owe a deep and abiding debt of gratitude to their predecessors for their courage, their foresight and their determination in being steadfast in their convictions and beliefs, for today, the Detroit Fire Fighters Association stands as a monument to their efforts.

...... M. M. Hollen

A Historical "First"

After 117 years as an all-male paid organization, the Detroit Fire Department graduated three women fire fighters from the Training Academy on September 30, 1977.

After completing an eight-week course of hauling ladders, heaving hose lines and scaling walls, Harriet Saunders, Sandy Kupper and Theresa Smith graduated along with 33 male fire fighters.

The girls were all assigned to engine companies to begin their four-month probationary tour of duty going on the city payroll at $14,727 a year. Harriet was assigned to Engine 21, Sandra to Engine 32 and Theresa to Engine 55.

The first women to qualify as fire fighters in Michigan's largest city. Left to right: Harriet Saunders, Sandy Kupper and Theresa Smith graduated from the Detroit Fire Department Training Academy on September 30, 1977. Proudly displaying their State and City training certificates the girls were assigned to engine companies to begin a four-month probationary tour of duty.

Fire Buffs Association

The Detroit Fire Buffs Association 1926 American LaFrance 1000 GPM "Metropolitan" Pumper was a familiar sight at fire service parades in the area for many years.

The Detroit Fire Buffs Association in 1977 begins its 40th year of service and support to the fire service of Metropolitan Detroit. Organized in 1937, this association of individuals and fire department members has functioned under three different names. It is interesting to note that four of the original eight charter members are still active in the organization today.

The Detroit Fire Buffs Association was founded under the name of the Fire Prevention Associates. Although a number of informal meetings had been held earlier, the Fire Prevention Associates held its first official meeting at the home of member Ray Carle on November 15, 1937. The highlight of the evening was listening for fire calls on a Detroit Police radio. Monthly meetings were subsequently held in various members' homes.

Late in 1939, the group changed its names to the Signal Club. The membership roster was extended to a maximum of 14. The club was disbanded at the outbreak of the Second World War. Upon cessation of hostilities, some of the original members, bolstered by members of the Auxiliary Firefighting Corps of the Detroit Fire Department, reactivated the club which was re-named the Detroit Fire Buffs Association. The group's purpose, however, remained unchanged: the advancement and promotion of ideas and experiences, and the cultivation of friendly social relations among those interested in fire prevention and suppression in the Metro Detroit area. The DFBA next became affiliated with the International Fire Buff Associates, an association of more than 70 fire buff clubs around the world.

The Detroit Fire Buffs continued to meet in members' homes and various fire houses from time to time, but in later years the group met in the old Lexington Hotel in the shadow of the General Motors Building In the early 1960's, the club purchased a 1926 American LaFrance pumper, which the members refurbished and made available for fire service parades and charity functions.

The 1908, Ahrens "Continental" steam pumper of Engine Co. No. 13, then located on the southeast corner of Russell St. & East Ferry. This was a second-size, 700 gpm. model and was built by the Ahrens Fire Engine Co. of Cincinnati, Ohio.

In 1966, the DFBA in conjunction with the city's other two fire buff clubs, co-hosted the Annual Convention of the International Fire Buff Associates in Detroit. During the civil disturbances that struck Detroit in 1967, DFBA members performed a number of non-firefighting services including communications, station watches and serving as "pilots" for out-of-town fire companies. In 1969 and 1970, club members took part in "Operation Safeguard", during the Hallowe'en period, when false alarms traditionally reached epidemic proportions. Volunteer crews of fire buffs and off-duty fire fighters manned unmarked department cars which responded to alarms in their assigned districts to determine if the alarm was malicious or for an actual fire. This saved the Detroit Fire Dept. hundreds of false alarm runs.

In recent years the DFBA has held its monthly meetings at the home of one of its life members, Albert J. Burch. The meeting room is a mini fire museum as well as the office of "The Visiting Fireman", an annual fire buff's directory that has long been considered the "Bible" of the fire buffing hobby.

This 1908 Ahrens of Engine 13 was discovered in a Pennsylvania museum and was returned to Detroit as a gift of the owner. The old engine last saw service in 1922 as a reserve unit and this photo taken in the Apparatus Shop shows the neglected condition it was in upon arrival. The Box 42 Associates volunteered to restore the engine and completed the task in 1973.

The Detroit Fire Buffs Association's current project is the raising of funds for the National Institute for Burn Medicine, as part of the Detroit Area Fire Buffs Association.

Charter members present for the original meeting of the Fire Prevention Associates in 1937, and still active in the Detroit Fire Buffs Association today include Ray A. Carles, Wilford A. Lindberg, Kenneth Koppitz and Edgar S. Dennison.

The Detroit Fire Buffs Association is proud of its history of service to the fire-fighting profession in this area, and hopes to continue to be of service for many years to come.

It had been 51 years since Detroiters last saw a horse drawn fire engine. Thousands of spectators were thrilled when this restored 1908 Ahrens engine made its appearance at the July, 1973 Firemen's Field Day at Tiger Stadium. See story on page 144.

Box 12 Associates

Box 12 Associates of Detroit was formed at a luncheon meeting in the then Book-Cadillac Hotel by Paxton Mendelssohn, a prominent Detroit businessman and financier and a handful of his friends who, to quote from his handwritten notes, "shared an interest in the Detroit Fire Department and in (the science of) fire fighting"

It was one of the first half dozen or so such groups formed in the United States. It was formed without charter or by-laws and with no political ties or interests, a situation existing to this day. Following three informal luncheon meetings at the Cadillac, the first official meeting of Box 12 Associates was held on February 1, 1927. Paxton Mendelssohn was elected chief, and there have been only two others elected to the post during the succeeding 50 years: Ivan Ludington, Sr., founder and president of the Ludington News Company, and the present chief, Glenn Bennett, head of security for the Michigan Consolidated Gas Company and former arson officer with the Detroit Fire Department.

The purpose of Box 12 today is unchanged from the concept established by Paxton Mendelssohn more than 50 years ago: A limited association of close friends whose principal avocation is to work for the betterment of the fire service, with particular emphasis on the Detroit Fire Department and the departments in the Detroit metro area. Many present and past officers of the Detroit and surrounding community fire departments have held or presently hold memberships in Box 12.

Meetings originally were held in the private homes of members, but in May, 1928 the official meetings were moved (for two years) to quarters in the Detroit-Leland Hotel. Meetings were subsequently held for three years at the Book-Cadillac Hotel before moving to quarters on LaSalle Boulevard for several years. Box 12 currently meets at noon on the third Wednesday of each month at the headquarters of the Ludington News Company on East Grand Boulevard in Detroit.

Box 42 Associates

Box 42 was formed in the early part of 1942 by a group of Auxilary Firemen at Engine Company 42. The name was chosen in respect and tribute to the firefighters of Engine Company 42, who unselfishly devoted their time and experience to the auxilaries' training.

Upon being phased out at the end of World War II, the auxiliaries decided to keep Box 42 alive and dedicated their services to assisting the Detroit Fire Department in various ways. The members take pride in their accomplishments in the public-relations area. One of their most visible projects was the restoration of old Engine 13, a 1908 Ahrens steam pumper, a job which took more than two and a half years. The horse drawn beauty is often seen at parades, musters, and the Field Day, and is a favorite of the crowds.

Currently, Box 42 is working on the cleaning, painting, and fixing-up of the former quarters of Engine 11 on Detroits' east side. When completed, the building will house the DFD museum. On display will be firematic items of historic interest, including the Ahrens steamer, and hopefully, an antique motorized rig or two.

Membership in the club stands at approximately forty, with about half of that number listed as active members. Throughout its existence, the club has awarded Life Membership to only three persons, two of whom are actively involved today. Ray Carle has registered the most service with the club, having become a member in 1945. Ray is the statistician and maintains extensive records of the department and of multiple-alarm fires dating back to his early days in the organization. He is a prominent member of all three Detroit area buff clubs.

Bill Lenaghan continued as an auxiliary firefighter in the DFD for many years and attained the rank of Auxiliary Battalion Chief. He also served as Fire Commissioner of Redford Township until his retirement. Besides his membership in Box 42, Bill stays involved in the Fire Service by his service to the Northville Township Fire Department.

The third life member was Retired DFD Battalion Chief Danny Sullivan, who passed away in 1970.

The individual interests within the group span a variety of specialties, including photography, communications, apparatus restoration and the like, but all share the common goal of supporting the Detroit Fire Department.

Department Chiefs

James
Battle

James
Elliott

John
Kendall

James
Broderik

William
McGraw

Timothy
Callahan

Edward
Meginnity

Stephen
DeMay

Michael
Callahan

Walter
Isreal

Alexander
Thompson

John
Keefe

John
Rourke

Hinnian
Higby

Edward
Blohm

Raymond
Vallad

Joseph
Adler

Laurance
Daly

Glenn
Thom

Charles
Quinlan

Lester
Emery

Joseph
Deneweth

Mahlon
Morowske

Samuel
Dixon

Donald
Robinson

The People

First Battalion

Nicholas Ackerman

Edward Alderman

Robert Alef

Edward Barbarich

James Barbarich

Joseph Boertmann

Alexander Boik

Richard Brown

Emilio Carlesimo

Jimmie Case

Harold
  Christensen

Charles Cramer

Louis Crist

Gerald Curley

Premo Damiani

Craig Desmet

Donald Dick

Johnnie Dillon

Robert Dixon

Danny Doell

James Eastin

Ernest Eschik

Raymond Fiddler

Wayne Fogle

Timothy Gable

Donald Galway

Charles Gatto

Hubert Gersch

Paul Green

Floyd Griem

Thomas Hart

Lon Hischke

Gary Hogg

Walter Horning

William Hudson

Raymond Husk

George Kelly

Andrew Jendrusina

Theodore Johnson

Thomas Jaminet

Wayne Isken

Charles Kersten

Andrew Kolar

Larry Koluch

Lawrence Kosmalski

Jack Krompatic

Gerald Lamb

Robert Lawrence

George Leone

Richard Loch

James Loehnis

Raymond Lybeer

Frank Maiorana

James Marshall

Isidoro Marrone

Donald McCosh

Robert McCarthy

Tawny McGowan

Michael McGraw

Alex Meldrum

Patrick Melady

Larry Miles

Kenneth Milliner

Daniel Moody

Edward Murray

Marcel Naert

Ralph Nelson

John Nyberg

William O'Dell

Larry Olson

Philip Pfahlert

Harold Pike

Colm Prentice

Michael Purcell

Donald Putrycus

William Quinn

James Rappert

Robert Rea

Richard
  Robertson

Robert Rosen

Thomas Rozandky

David Sandora

Henry Scheel

Jack Seely

Kenneth Seipke

John Siegel

Marion Sims

Ralph Slezak

Dennis Slowke

Jay Smith

Julius Sobonya

Paul Stieber

Joseph Svabik

Francis Szczesny

Van Tatum

Charles Towne

John Tucker

Edward Tujaka

Patrick Tutak

Arthur Tygard

Marcus Urban

Alfred Ventre

Robert Vissotski

Rudolph Wagner

Edwin Ward

Percy Warmack

Albert Wells

Marshall Wesley

Bryant Williams

Thomas Wojkiewicz

Donald Wolf

Marquis Wooden

Walter Woodrow

Raymond Zaborski

Allan Zadrowski

Eugene Zykewski

Leonard Zembrzuski

Hercules Jefferson

Frank Szopko

Second Battalion

John Antoniotti
Donald Asbill
Richard Avey
John Bastien
Marvin Beatty

Nelson Belanger
Pete Benenati
Robert Carpenter
Thomas Cavanaugh
Joseph Charette

Gary Clapp
Lawrence Cubitt
Ronald Davis
Norman Degen
Andrew Dempsey

Francis Dostert
William Douras
David Edwards
William Fairweather
Stanley Fisher

Herbert Hahn
George Heidelmeyer
Barry Hendra
Steven Hoffman
Byron Hotchkiss

Frank Jachym
Leroy Jenkins
Thomas Kaluzny
Albert Kasper
Charles Kelly

Francis Kelly

Michael Kish

Michael Kokocinski

Joseph Krolik

Gerald Linlow

Adrian Locke

Kenneth Loffman

Pedro Lopez

Donald Lowe

Gerald Luczak

F. Madden

Richard Maher

Michael Markowski

Raymond Maurer

Francis McGarry

Larry McNeill

Raymond Miller

Richard Nagy

William Nicholas

Edward Nowinski

Thomas O'Bryan

James O'Hara

Theodore Panaretos

Stephen Parsell

Russell Pauling

Wesley Pincheck

Frank Polk

Bernard Quinn

Louis Riley

Daniel Rooks

Paul Schimeck

Larry Sefton

Paul Sevald

Richard Shinske

Michael Simon

Robert Skonieski

Gordon Smith

Dennis Smoot

Carl Sokoloski

Robert Swickard

Clyde Tome

John Urbin

John Vantiem

Loray Welch

Billy Williams

Emil Magier

John Wisniewshi

William Wolfe

Third Battalion

Patrick Adams

Raymond Andrzejak

Andrew Angelucci

Russell Arbuckle

Joseph Baleda

Eugene Barterian

Raymond Barr

Frank Bauer

Francis Becigneul

Robert Bradley

Thomas Breitschuh

Ken Brosowski

Thomas Buckley

Henry Cairo

Leo Calabro

Howard Carlson

Thomas Carter

Paul Castone

Ronald Ceckowski

Joseph Cernava

Walter Chapman

John Chakan

Dennis Chojnacki

Samuel Cimino

Lloyd Cummins

Thaddeus Czeski

John Davis

George Debruyne

Frank DeMaggio

Don Denys

159

Jules Deschryver

Guenther Dey

Anthony Doemer

Stanley Durecki

Timothy Eklund

Fred Emke

Dominic Fantauzzo

Dennis Fett

Lawrence Foshey

Fred Fuqua

Timothy Gajewski

Robert Gallmore

William Garden

Raymond George

Edwin Gersch

Charles Gerardy

David Goldsmith

Earl Grill

Albert Gruber

John Gusumano

William Hartnup

Lawrence Harp

James Jagger

Raymond Kapcia

Daniel Katchmark

Joseph Keith

Stanley Keitz

Herbert Kennedy

Paul Keyes

Richard Knobelsdorf

Richard Knott

Thaddeus Kotula

Kenneth Kovach

Barry Lebeau

Gary Lee

Richard Lohmann

William Loranger

Carl Luttenbacher

Donald Lyon

John MacEwan

Raymond MacShara

Charles Marble

Warner Matchull

Allen McDonald

Alexander Merkau

Walter Meyers

William Miller

William Miller

Jeffrey Mortier

Steven Morant

Billy Napier

Richard Narduzzi

Robert Nash

Howard Neidermeier

Edward Netzel

Alfred Neumann

Charles Nikkila

Bernard O'Grady

Pete Pink

Wayne Piotrowski

Vincenzu Pozzuoli

Donald Purdue

John Reip

Robert Riopelle

Karl Ryan

Jerry Sample

Clyde Sanders

George Schwanitz

Raymond Schiepke

Thomas Schreiber

Victor Seipke

Donald Sewell

Edward Shiner

Everett Shirley

Gerald Smith

Dennis Smith

Daune Smith

Edward Stephens

Jack Stelzer

Raymond Storms

Robert Strang

Joseph Szymaszek

Robert Teipel

Clarence Tobias

Frank Torrice

Robert Trombley

Edward Veda

Tomas Velthuysen

Arthur Versace

Michael Votta

Richard Waem

William Weinert

Dennis Welcher

William Wilson

Major Winston

Paul Yeip

Daniel Ziegeler

Fourth Battalion

John Anderson

David Battishill

Albert Belloli

Edwin Biebel

Glenn Blank

Billy Blackwell

Richard Bokuniewicz

David Bragg

Francis Broderick

John Brycz

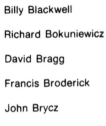     

George Burke

Carl Byrum

Gordon Campbell

Dennis Cannon

Richard Carter

Louis Cardinale

Malcolm Carr

Thomas Charron

James Coles

Walter Cook

Charles Cooper

Edward Cooney

Richard Cronk

Richard Decker

Michael Demkowicz

Ray Dettloff

James Divozzo

Lee Dodson

George Dohring

Alexander Drozdowicz

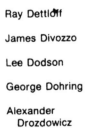     

Eugene Durand

Larry Eklund

John Foley

Sims Friday

Martin Gascon

Robert Goik

Larry Gordon

Raymond Grabowski

Ronald Grden

Alphonse Green

Richard Griese

Ronald Haas

Jerry Haney

Leonard Henzi

Jerry Janosky

Calvin Johnson

Thomas Johnson

William Jones

Thaddeus Kajder

Ken Koch

Richard Kostrzewski

Mark Lafferty

Dennis Lecuyer

Dennis Leonard

Michael Linck

Daniel MacArthur

John Maher

Harry Manuel

Richard Martin

Michael McArthey

Elmer McFadden

Roger Mertz

Patrick Mesko

Keith Miner

James Monahan

Robert Mowatt

Clifford Murphree

William O'Grady

James Offner

Albert Olin

Robert Panzica

David Pegg

Rocco Perretta

Edward Peterson

Edward Powers

Mark Rebrovich

Arthur Ricker

John Roodbeen

James Samuels

James Sanders

William Schnars

Gary Siuru

George Smith

Gerald Spinelli

Edward Sternicki

Joseph St. John

Robert Tighe

John Tomas

Dennis Trombley

Marvin Ureel

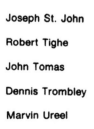     

William Walker

Charles Webb

Marshall Wimberly

Herman Worthy

Michael Yeager

Clarence Zdanowski

Roy Harrington

Fifth Battalion

Mitchell Ashman
William Ashford
Leonard Bartlett
Eldon Beckwith
George Bednar

Gregory Best
Jerome Beyer
Don Bloom
Leo Brink
Roy Brogan

Walter Brown
Charlie Brown
Chester Buckholtz
Dan Bucacink
James Bush

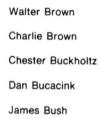    

Robert Carr
Mark Carpenter
Timothy Cashen
Raymond Cashen
Evaristo Cervantes

Rudolfo Cervantes
Douglas Childs
Edward Clancy
Lawrence Colombo
Gerald Corey

Donald Cronin
John Dawson
Arthur Dodds
Edwin Dziuban
Edwin Filas

Bruce Finney

Keith Fleming

Serge Foresi

George Gehling

Julius Glab

Dale Grable

James Griffin

Paul Gross

James Grzelewski

Herschel Hembree

John Hemeyer

Robert Hogans

James Hogg

William Hynes

Daniel Isakson

Harold Jackson

Carl Jarema

Donald Johnson

Douglas Johnston

Ronald Jones

Lowell Koontz

Emory Kramp

David Kruger

Robert Latka

Melvin Leskie

Albert Lloyd

Waymon Lollar

Melvin Lowery

John McCann

Timothy McConnell

William McEwan
James McMahan
James Means
Roy Messink
Douglas Metcalf

Martin Moro
Ronald Mortiere
Ken Murawski
Donald Neill
Paul Nettles

Patrick O'Brien
Camillo Opipari
Douglas Paul
Lawrence Paul
Samuel Payton

John Pike
Bruce Porter
Leroy Price
Nick Reghi
Albert Richardson

Danny Riggs
Robert Roths
Ken Rothermel
Kenneth Routin
Joseph Ryan

John Ryan
Michael Sabbath
Earl Sanders
Larry Sanders
Earl Sanders

Thomas Schaecher

Jerry Smith

Norman Smith

Lawrence Snowden

Leroy Szarafinski

Kenneth Tafts

Iver Thornburg

Daniel Tinney

Ralph Van Sickle

Harold Watkins

Marion Wells

Willie Wilkerson

Gerald Wilson

Mark Wilson

Stanley Zell

 Steven House

Sixth Battalion

Samuel Abdelnour

Thomas Andre

Thomas Arnold

Ellison Ashe

Richard Baumann

Leonard Beard

Kenneth Brining

Jimmie Brown

Robert Brumm

Rolland Brunke

John Bullo

Neil Bushong

William Bush

Daniel Byrge

William Carr

Robert Cherro

Larry Crowder

David Culkowski

Albert Darden

Thomas DeCoster

Norman Defour

George Demres

Dennis Dermidoff

Raymond Donaldson

Donald Dorey

Jonathan Doty

Bernard Dozek

David Engelhardt

Frank English

Edward Essian

Robert Evans

Charles Ferguson

Salvatore Finazzo

Robert Fournier

Jack Fritsch

Wilbur Garrison

John Gerhardt

Gordon Giganic

William Girardin

Charles Grabman

Donald Hagen

Harley Hagerman

Raymond Hamm

Jack Hansen

Robert Hasten

William Holleran

Marion Hollen

Johnny Jackson

Roger Johnston

Bertil Johansson

Dennis Klimek

Donald Knobelsdorf

Michael Kostich

Don Koster

Ronald Kreuser

Paul Langlois

Donald Lebeau

Alex Leme

Julian Lepoudre

Robert Linder

Gary Lobes

Charles Lockridge

Vernon Loepp

Frank Lorkowski

Henry Maciejewski

Allan Maiorana

Mike Martin

Michael Mason

Michael Mason

Dale McDonald

Larry McDonald

Marvin McLean

Edwin Michael

Neal Miller

David Milam

Robert Molnar

John Moore

Hillary Murray

Glenn Murray

Kenneth Murray

Ronald Naumann

George Nikoriuk

Martin O'Brien

Michael Órlowski

Leo Panagos

Edward Pas

Edward Pastucha

Donald Porrett

Henry Potrykus

Edward Pressel

William Ptak

Clarence Raymond

Roger Reeves

Albert Reynaert

John Richter

Harold Ring

Edward Riopelle

Robert Riopelle

Robert Rolf

Frank Rossi

Ludwig Ruprecht

Arthur Saumier

Frederick Schwartz

David Shepherd

Larry Shumaker

James Slaton

Edward Smith

Chester Smith

Edward Smith

Paul Sny

Norman Tenhopen

Leo Teschendorf

Leonard Trawczynski

John Trombley

Peter Tybinka

Albert Vidosh

Charles Vought

Harold Vreeland

Thomas Walker

James Wandrie

Paul Weber

Joy Whitford

William Whitcher

Charles Williams

Denis Wittig

John Fusting

Robert Williams

Seventh Battalion

Casimer Badynee

William Barkell

Gerald Baxter

Dennis Benton

Peter Benskey

Robert Bias

Raymond
  Birmingham

Louis Bitten

Clarence Bolda

Albert Brachulis

Robert Brady

Thomas Brown

William Brock

Terrence Browne

Harlan Brown

David Buckwitz

Gerald Butler

Michael Chaney

Norman Colembei

Michael Collins

Larry Cooper

Guy Cooper

Joseph Daniel

Ronald Daniels

Laverne Dinatale

Robert Dombrowski

David Dziuban

Conrad Evans

Raymond Faulk

James Foote

Edmund Forys

Gary Foreman

Robert Franquist

Charles Galbraith

Ronald Gapa

Edmund Gawenda

David Gerometta

Larry Gilmer

James Gilmore

Raymond
  Grochowski

C. Gurski

Louis Gusoff

Robert Haig

William Hallmark

James Handzlik

Douglas Heit

Rudy Hertlein

Richard Hoffman

James Jackson

George Decaussin

Larry Jenkins

Robert Johnson

Dennis Kelly

Carroll Kingins

Wilbur Klann

Ronald Kolenda

Eugene Kotlinski

Frank Kotlarek

Harry Krzyawiak

Edward Kwiatkowski

Richard Latka

Roger Leppala

James Lewis

Wilbert Lewis

Frank Lis

John Lisuk

Samuel Locke

Jack Loomis

Larry Lorenz

Thomas Magro

George Main

Carl Mansfield

Charles Master

Michael McDonald

John McGraw

Thomas McInchak

Raymond Michalski

Ronald Michalik

William Mills

Michael Mlinarich

Edward Moros

Frank Nettleton

Kent Nicholson

Johnny O'Dell

Benjamin Patterson

Paul Payne

Donald Pemmitt

Enrique Perez

Dean Pierce

Gary Potvin

Kenneth Quincy

David Ratcliff

Harold Reese

Richard Regnier

Ralph Rehmer

Thomas Riley

J. Roman

Andrew Rushford

William Russell

Robert Sanderson

Sylvester Sartin

Donald Schultz

Robert Sheehan

Thomas Shirley

Edward Smith

John Stout

Joseph Strach

Ronald Todd

Robert Van Buhler

Archie Warde

Ronald Whitaker

Robert Williams

Carl Williams

Ron Winchester

Daniel Zinser

Joseph Zyla

Wesley Paciorka

Charles Fisher

Eighth Battalion

Stephen Adamczyk

Leonard Balcer

Jerry Billings

Henry Boroski

William Boren

France Bowers

Glenn Breuhan

Kenneth Casterlow

Raymond Cavin

Raymond Chance

Joseph Croteau

George Daum

Herbert Decker

Michael Dell

John Downey

Thomas Doyle

Daniel Drewek

Michael Duhonich

William Dunn

Donald Edge

Curtis Edmonds

Jerry Edwards

Wayne Elkins

Elias Elkouri

Raymond Eskau

Robert Faigle

Frank Fields

John Foydel

Raymond Gatzke

181

Donald Morris

William Myatt

Douglas Naas

John Nizol

James Olson

    (row 1)

Zigmund Orzech

Joseph Pantano

Charles Patreka

Cleveland Price

Charlie Pritchett

     (row 2)

Donald Ross

Paul Sanders

Ralph Sharp

David Shaw

Herbert Silver

     (row 3)

Don Simmons

Thomas Smith

Norman Speier

Chester Stuch

Thomas Suchora

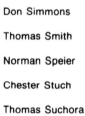      (row 4)

Walter Thursam

Vincent Ventimiglia

Joseph Tomakowski

Ernest Tor

David Vann

     (row 5)

Charles Vorpagel

Robert Wallington

Charles Weir

Lester Weil

John Weingart

     (row 6)

Joseph Godell

Edward Green

Robert Gulley

John Gusler

Elmer Hammond

Robert Hawthorne

Harold Heikkila

Anthony Jackson

Byron Jackson

Dennis Jaissle

Gary Johnson

Michael
 Kaczorowski

Monroe Kelley

Robert Kochler

William Koehler

Thomas Koehler

John Konsek

Raymond Lanzi

Gary Lincoln

Roy Lozon

Gerald Lubig

Walter Lukasiak

Reide MacKenzie

Robert Malie

Roger Mathews

Timothy McHale

Lawrence Milke

Thomas Monks

Douglas Moore

Glenn Morris

Fain White

Adrian Williams

Andy Wilburn

Robert Wiltsie

George Wright

Michael Zunich

Gilbert Able

Ninth Battalion

Tony Amato

Reginald Amos

Larry Andersen

John Arasim

James Archibald

William Armstrong

Edward Audet

James Bassett

Murray Bates

George Bell

Ronald Bell

Gary Bonine

Joseph Bozich

Robert Brown

Delmar Brown

David Browne

Gordon Brown

Frank Bungert

Thomas Campanella

David Carlen

Joseph Celice

John Chester

James Choike

Kenneth Clark

Harold Clynick

Ralph Conti

Jerry Cook

Samuel Cox

Nicholas Cretu

Charles Curry

Ronald Favors

Harold Fisher

Wade Forshee

Brian Fox

Thomas Francis

Paul Garrison

Charles Gay

Patrick Gayney

Gregory Gerling

Clarence Gibson

Robert Grutza

Charles Harris

Claude Hollisten

Albert Hood

Van Horton

Napoleon Howard

Edward Huyck

Glennie Johnson

Michael Johnson

Anthony Joyce

Gerald Kanopsky

Richard Kaufmann

Gerald Klassa

Joseph Konfara

Joseph Labbe

Earl Lange

Donald Manley

Marvin Massey

Joseph Mazzoline

Courtland
  McDonald

James Mimanaugh

Gerald Mitchell

Richard Moller

Rayford Moody

John Morgan

Philip Moranty

Gregory Navarre

Gary Norfleet

Billie Nunnery

John O'Grady

Stanley Osowski

Ray Owens

Robert Pepper

Gordon Pierce

Lawrence Pilut

David Raley

Michael Rapach

Joseph Robinson

Carl Rugenski

Albert Ryans

Edward Sadlowski

Thomas Samueloff

Joseph Schweyer

Leo Selasky

George Sevald

Vander Shepherd

James Shriber

Johnny Sims

Ronald Sipperley

Charles Smith

Joseph Smigielski

Eugene Snarski

Ronald Stokes

Julius Streety

John Sullivan

Harvey Theibert

Frederick Thiel

Ronny Tonti

Robert Waltower

Eric West

Robert
  Wielzorkowski

Ralph Williams

Harry Wilson

Joseph Wilson

Robert Wilson

John Wilson

Chester Zgoda

Tenth Battalion

Albert Abdullah

Robert Amoe

Raymond Augustyn

Harold Barnes

Darryl Binder

Earl Bodenhorn

Gerald Boelstler

Jon Bozich

George Bray

Ernest Breitschuh

Harry Brown

Ronald Bussell

Henry Cairo

Luigi Cicchelli

William Courneya

Robert Decaussin

Dennis Declark

Joseph Dickerson

George Doebler

John Dubrawski

Norbert Dysarz

Eugene Falbo

James Federoff

Edward Ferguson

James Fillmore

Phillip Friday

Ralph Gardner

Armando Gennari

Robert Gotelaere

William Greenan

189

Randy Gurnack
Adam Hagen
Robert Hallman
Robert Hill
Robert Hlatky

Arnold Holmes
Lemuel Hoover
Raymond Huck
Michael Hunt
Leon Jackson

John Kleiner
Arthur Kowalske
Norbert Kurzawa
Richard Lancaster
David Lau

Melvin Lesnau
Roger Lesniak
John Leverington
Alan Lorenger
Hugh MacDonald

Dennis Masty
George Matthews
Eugene McCarthy
Gene McDonald
James McPhee

Robert Meldrum
Carl Melchior
Roy Miller
Madison Moore
Fred Nazar

Kelly Norris

James O'Grady

Lawrence Orlando

Richard Osentoski

David Palm

Charles Phipps

Joseph Plonkey

Thomas Racosta

Richard Rail

Donald Reusch

Peter Reyes

Jerome Reynaert

David Richie

Martin Robinson

Adam Ross

Dell Small

Marcell Smagghe

Joseph Smith

Martin Snarski

Anthony Spezia

Frank Spilitener

Jim Spry

Robert Stevens

Richard
  Stirzinger

Glenn Stock

Kenneth Swistock

William Taube

Donald Thomas

Raymond Timmer

Jimmie Tophan

Christopher Towne

Anthony Trupiano

John Turner

Michael Turner

Arthur Tyll

Brian Uhl

George Warzyniak

Aaron Watkins

Jimmie Weidemanr

Joseph Wojcik

Richard Woodbury

Don Yaden

Ronald Yokubison

George Younan

Edward Zablocki

Russ Zitzmann

John Gargulinski

Stanley Stone

Donald Desjardins

Eleventh Battalion

Raymond Alverson

Thomas Baggot

Gerald Baggot

Terry Barker

Tobie Barksdale

George Bartley

Bernard Beaton

Vincent Beale

Robert Berchem

Earl Berry

Robert Bonner

John Boss

Edward Brazen

Robert Brown

Norman Brown

Kenneth Brown

John Cadenink

Robert Cadaret

Gerald Carlan

Larry Carlisle

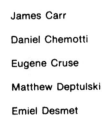

James Carr

Daniel Chemotti

Eugene Cruse

Matthew Deptulski

Emiel Desmet

Joseph Diefenbach

Francis Dolan

Donald Donati

John Dougherty

Mario Fontana

Gregory Foresi

Noah Fowlkes

Douglas Fox

William Frank

Robert Frost

Theodore Giguere

Jack Graves

James Harris

Michael Hastings

William Hausch

Thomas Hegarty

Richard Hendrian

Donald Hendricks

Thomas Holt

John Hynes

William Irwin

Clyde Jaynes

William Johnson

John Johnston

Robert Jones

William Juergens

Frank Kanopsky

Joseph Kelemen

Donald Klann

Barney Knorp

Gerald Kolenda

Ervin Koshen

James Kovach

Royal Kretschmer

William Laprise

Roger Legris

William Lindow

Ervin Love

James Lynch

Donald MacIntyre

Robert Madlinger

Dennis McClure

Frederick McKay

John McPhail

William Megis

Gary Mitchell

Frank Morandy

Richard Morris

Thomas Mosteiko

John Mueller

Fred Neal

Frederick
  Nicholls

Thomas O'Neill

Duane Olander

Anthony Ounanian

Gregory Pope

James Porter

Joseph Portelli

Wesley Radford

Kelvin Roberts

Leo Semigan

James Siebert

Alan Silver

James Steffke

James Stockton

Richard Summers

James Szafran

Frank Tata

John Tederington

Richard Teefey

James Tonti

Waldo Valdez

Jeff Van Every

Russell Van Sickle

Robert Walter

Gerald Ward

Frederick Wasser

George Wood

George Gehling

Kenneth Gabriel

EMS

Gwendolyn Alexander

Rodney Allen

Mabel Anderson

Raymond Atrasz

Robert Barnhart

Bruce Bay

Samuel Beglin

John Berry

Arthur Blum

Daniel Bojalad

Carl Boldon

Raymond Bradley

William Brem

Dale Britt

Daniel Brown

John Bryant

Henry Buford

Barbara Bynum

Joseph Callahan

Mary Campbell

Cheryl Campbell

Lawrence Campbell

Michaek Ciaramitaro

Michael Cloyd

Denise Cobb

Gary Coomer

Charles Corley

Tom Court

Willard Crawford

Thomas Crooks

197

John Crowley
Archie Crump
James Custer
Gerald Dajnowkz
Wanzie Davis

Robert Deblock
Gregory Decker
John Densmore
Alvin DePriest
Richard Dolley

Cynthis Dotson
Jesse Dunn
Nora Earhart
Timothy Ellison
Clara Ellington

William Farmer
Glenda Farmer
Terry Fenner
Charles Finley
Patrick Flannery

Darryl Ford
Robert Foster
Richard Frank
Tyrione Freeman
Gary Fromius

Samuel Gazzarato
Walter Godzwon
Alvin Gordon
Philip Gorka
Jimmie Granger

William Green

Terry Harriman

Gail Hawkins

Bruce Henderson

Henry Hicks

James Hill

Thomas Hirsch

Don Hobbs

Shilako Holiness

Eugene Holmes

Terry Hudson

Richard Hughes

Donald Hutchison

Richard Iacovacci

Robert Jackson

Celestine Jackson

Robin Jaynes

Lucius Jeffries

Andrew Johnson

Ellanor Johnson

Denise Jones

Bruce Jones

Rance Jones

Andrew Karlin

Jeffrey Keeton

Velma Kelley

Gary Kelly

Michael Kempton

Scott Kloian

Bartholomew Kocik

Charles Labash

Dennis Laforest

Gayle Lawlor

Leslie Lennier

Fred Leopold

Taras Lichonczak

Wilson Lightfoot

Michael Lucero

Wayne Lun

Charles Mack

Jimmie Malone

Daniel Markham

James Marshall

Allen Mays

Peggy McCary

Mildred McClary

Wilson McCrackin

Carl Melchior

Gerald
 Merriweather

Eric Michalke

William Miller

Michael Mooney

Steven Morawiec

Herbert Moss

Kevin Mullane

Leonard Muss

Joseph Myers

James Neal

David Nelson

Robert Nilsen

Dennis Nilsen

Portia Norris

Robert Parks

Bryant Parrish

Richard Patrick

Casey Perryman

Bernist Plair

Louis Poole

Johnnie Powell

John Price

Jesse Pulliam

John Rargowski

Arthur Robinson

John Robinson

Bernard Samet

David Schneider

Dave Sharpy

John Sharpley

Reginald Shepherd

Dennis Shropshire

Kurt Sielaff

Alvin Smith

Rosetta Smith

Bernice Smith

Edward Smith

David Stanton

Ronald Stavale

Delores Stewart

Christopher
    Stephen

Henry Stitzman

201

Sandra Stone

Kay Tallman

John Telck

Dave Teske

Timothy Thomson

Michael Tiedeck

Robert Tobin

Jack Trueman

Tehran Tucker

Vasil Tulicea

Mark
  Vanderstraeten

Leroy
  Vickerstaff

Russell Wallison

Danny Warren

William Watters

Thomas Weakley

Preston West

James Wettegren

David Whitmore

Michael White

Carl Whitmore

Clarence Williams

Wilson Williams

James Wilson

Robert Bye

Administration And Central Office

Melvin Jefferson

Phillip Gorak

Theo Phillips

Robert Case

Lawrence Rivard

Deljeana Barber

Ethel Brown

Gloria Crockett

Patricia Dziuba

Henry Edwards

George Johnson

June Jones

Mosetta Jones

Betty Korff

Marianne Hoske

Louis Oldani

Arlene Trice

Marvin William

Margaret Williams

Chester Wilson

Joseph Zdilla

Communications Division

James Deneweth

Patricia Fane

Alvin Fisher

Abner Garrett

Robert Grandy

Robert
  Gumbleton

Larry Hoover

Diane Jones

Muirlene Jones

Earl Joyner

Donald Koch

Dennis Koker

Richard Langrell

Ronald Mertz

Wallace Nissle

Frank Pospiech

Elanor Ridley

Alson Robinson

Maurice Roche

Robert Saydak

Orville
  Schudlich

Matthew Smith

Lorraine Thomas

Beatrice Traylor

John Vekoff

Shirley Whitlow

Charles Ziegenbein

Donald Ziolkowski

Fire Marshal Division

Walter Bailey

Rayo Baker

Harold Berry

Clarence Black

Horace Bogan

William Bradley

Gerald Brills

Sarah Burks

Patricia Davis

Donald Dibble

Albina Franczak

Dennis Holland

Donald Gallagher

Ameen Haamid

Toney Hughes

Lewis Jaissle

Dorothy King

Robert Kuntz

Stephen Krupa

Richard Lang

Paul Lee

Vera Mikolow

James Millimer

Robert Michalik

Mujahid
   Malik-Ul-Mulk

Victor Nevin

O'Dell Parker

Cynthia Peck

Charles Ramsey
Donald Robinson
Edward Sarzynski
Herman Sewick
Lynette Sims

Carleton Smith
Leonard Struthers
Ralph Sheiring
Edward Zaremba
Henry Turner

Leonard Uschwald
John Vanden Boom
Patricia Wanetick
Quinton Watkins
Kenneth Wellman

Arson

Michael
  Buschbacher

Jerome Boyer

Conrad Bist

John Beyer

Charles Craft

Charles Evancho

James Kitson

Robert McClary

Marvin Monroe

Timothy Reghi

Donald Robinson

Herman Rubarth

John Yurko

Apparatus Division

William Arnold

Charles Babinger

Edward Battle

Robert Bellmay

William Bell

George Blackburn

Carolyn Braggs

Bernard Bretz

Phillip Budnik

Jenice Burney

Robert Brodeur

James Cartwright

Hollis Cogborn

Hugh Dial

Karl Doppelberger

Earl Drew

Samuel Dunnell

James Elliott

Daniel Epperson

Robert Felix

George
  Garabedian

Clarence
  Gilginas

Marvin Graves

William Harper

Kenneth Hill

Matthew Holowach

Jerry Land

Norman Kossak

David Kopp

Thomas Kniaz

Gerald Johnson

Ronald Houle

Joseph Lutfy

Robert McGee

Ivan Ozment

Joseph
  Richardson

Derrick Rogers

William Ruth

Louis Scheich

Urian Payne

Leonard Pope

Arnet Streeter

Paul Snyder

Chris Snell

James Smith

Joseph
  Schaldewbrawd

Frederick Thayer

Eleazar Shepherd

John Searcy

Creston Wolfe

Arthur Velasco

Michael McComskey

Others

Suzanne Bielski

Vera Fisher

James Merlo

Monta Meixsell

David Connelly

James Burton

Willis Jackson

Elizabeth Thomas

George Ufford

Herbert Holcomb

Robert Koster

Sherman Town

James Adams

Ruth Campbell

Rebecca Tinsley

Samuel Dixon

John King

Gerald Stesiak

Jerrold Apel

David Angeleri

Narvie Fair

William Foster

Charley Steel

Joseph Boland

Joseph Paquin

Myrtle Allen

Daniel Bushey

David Alexander

Bill Eisner

Clarence Woodard

Retired Members

Marion Cassar

Phyllis Koesar

Joseph Adler

Fritz Beer

Edward Blohm

Manley Cool

Bernard Decoster

Joseph Deneweth

Lester Emery

Arthur Fischer

John Hedgcock

Bessie Kaplan

Gerald Montgomery

Albert Noel

Charles Quinlan

Frank Saims

Eleanore Schudlich

Ray Valad

211

Firehouses

Ryan & Hildale

Livernois & Curtis

Lakepointe & Whittier

Hoover & Manning

Coplin, N. of Jefferson

E. Jefferson & Hart

Lafayette & Mt. Elliott

Lafayette & St. Antoine

Lafayette & St.
Antoine

Miller & Helen

East Warren &
Rohns

Shoemaker &
French Rd.

Mt. Elliott & E.
Davison

Russell & Wilkins

Alexandrine, W. of
Cass

Second & Burroughs

Byron & Taylor

Linwood & Calvert

Twelfth & La Belle

West Warren & Lawton

Milwaukee & Riopelle

Bayside & Sanders

Grand River & Trinity

Curtis & Fenmore

Ladder 26
    & Engine 54

Meyers & Florence

Detroit City Airport

Houston-Whittier & Gratiot

Greenfield & Fenkell

Washington Blvd. & Larned

West Gd. Blvd. & Cobb Pl.

West Chicago & Livernois

Livernois, S. of Walton

Bagley & Sixth

Byron & Taylor (EMS No. 1)

Kenilworth, E. of Woodward

Mc Graw & Martin

Lafayette & Lawndale

W. Jefferson & Solvay

East Gd. Blvd. & Moran

Park & Montcalm

Russell & Erskine
(Old Ladder 5)

Engine 46

Grace & Knoddell

St. Jean, N. of Mack

West Lafayette & 10th

Central & Dix

Junction & Rogers

Michigan, E. of Military

West Gd. Blvd. & Vinewood

Engine 55 & Ladder 27
Loc.: Joy Rd. & Ashton

Engine 52 & Ladder 31
Loc.: Manistique & E. Warren

Crane & Brinket

Burt Rd. & Schoolcraft

Mt. Elliott & Sylvester

Gratiot & Grandy
(DFD Historical Museum,
now on the National
Register of Historical
Places)

Seven Mile & John R.

Engine 44 & Ladder 18

Award Winning Photos
Of Joseph Mancinelli

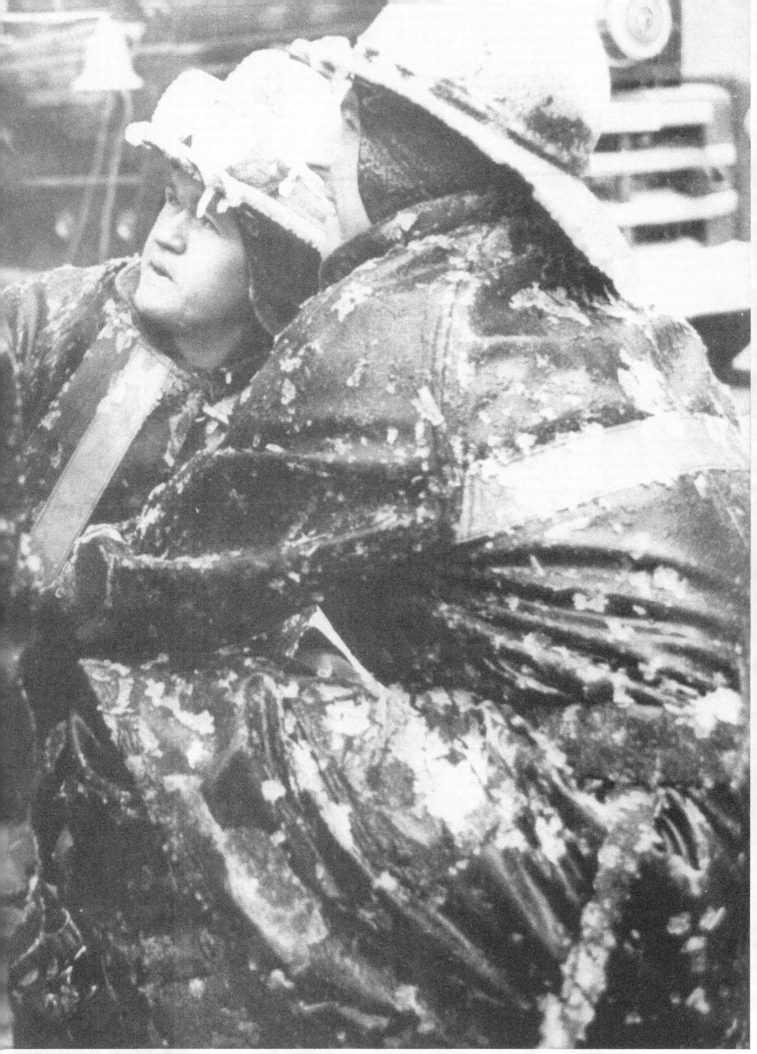

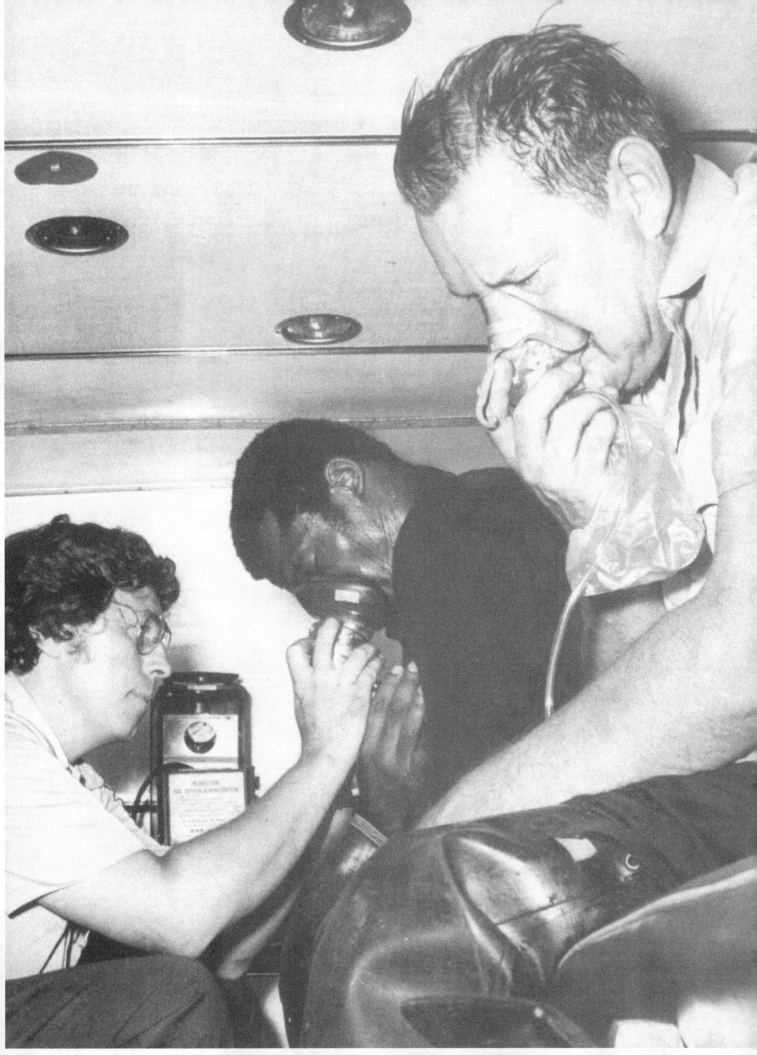

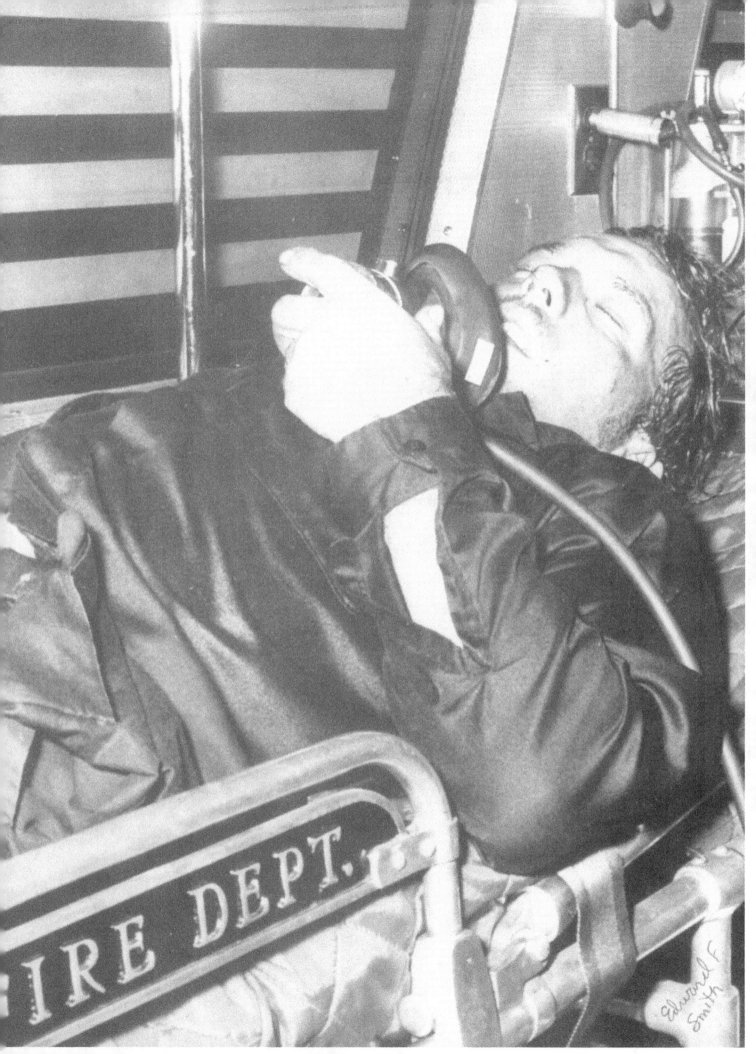

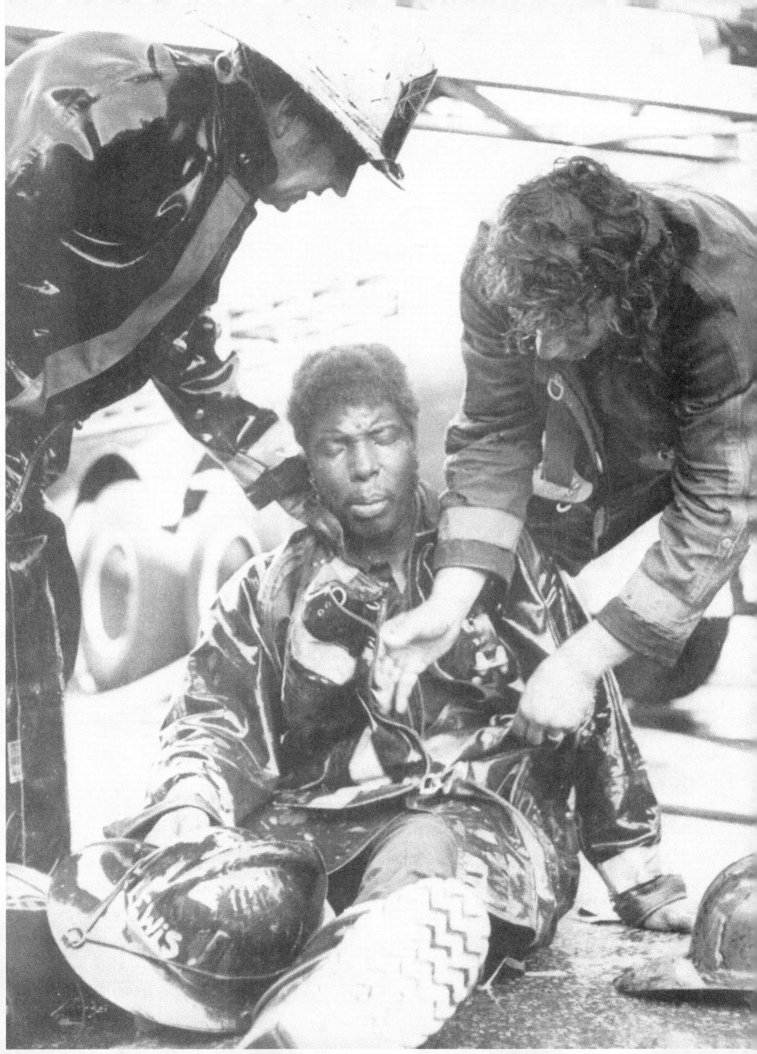

Prize Photos Of
Bill Eisner

When preparing a book of this kind a cut off date must be agreed upon after which no updating because of changes in personnel or in titles can be made, however during the preparation of this history, two of our brothers lost their lives in the line of duty and we would be remiss if they were not specially remembered herein.

CURTIS RANDOLPH

July 24, 1955 - Oct. 29, 1977

Curtis Randolph, a probationary Fire Fighter of Engine 32 lost his life in a flash of flame and smoke when caught in a back-draft while fighting a one-alarm house fire in a vacant dwelling at 1601 Lillibridge Avenue.

The tragedy which took the life of Randolph, first black fire fighter to be killed in action, also injured six fellow firemen. The blaze determined to be arson after an extensive investigation resulted in two persons being charged with the crime.

MICHAEL L. JOHNSON

Sept. 27, 1945 - Dec. 12, 1977

Firefighter Michael L. Johnson, a 4½ year veteran of the Department was killed when his head struck a ceiling beam as he tillered Ladder 11 out of its quarters at E. Milwaukee and Riopelle while responding to a box alarm.

Ladder 11, a 1977 Seagrave, 100 foot aerial, boasted a closed, heated tiller cab. (Ladder 1, pictured on page is a similar truck)

It is presumed that Johnson raised up from his tiller seat to don or adjust his fire coat after having given the driver the signal to proceed.

Inspector Barney H. Wasowicz

With the retirement of Barney Wasowicz in June, 1976, the Fire Department Photo Lab was officially closed. Inspector Wasowicz, of the Fire Marshal Division, on assignment to the Photo Lab started his career in 1951 as a Fire Fighter assigned to Engine 12. Most of Barney's Fire Fighting days were spent at Ladder Co. 27, between 1954 and 1966. In September of 1966 he was transferred to the Fire Marshals Division and a year later promoted to Fire Prevention Inspector.

Shortly after being detailed to the Phot Lab Barney was one of the first photographers on the scene at the July, 1967 civil disturbance on Twelfth St. taking numerous pictures of the fires in the area. Inspector Wasowicz was the first to introduce color photography in the Department along with developing techniques, many of the fine fire photos in this book are Barney's work. Wasowicz also took all the photographs which appeared on the I.D. cards of the Fire Department.

Inspector Wasowicz received two Department citations during his career and completed many assignments above and beyond the call of duty. Many of Barney's outstanding photographs will become a part of the colorful history of the Detroit Fire Department.

Joe Mancinelli

In October, 1951, having heard of his photographic background and having a need for a photographer, Fire Marshal Edward Hall invited Joseph Mancinelli, then a three year Fire Fighter assigned to Engine 32, to transfer to the Fire Marshal Divison as a Fire Prevention Inspector with the understanding that Joe would be his photographer as needed. Joe accepted the challange and remained a part time photographer for 10 years.

In 1961, Joe was assigned full time to the photo lab and placed on 24 hour call, responding to "extras", arson cases, vehicle accidents, and when ever needed.

In 1965 the Photography Section was created by executive order and Joe was the logical choice to head up this new Section.

Joe has received 21 awards for his fire pictures, one of which was a first place award. His pictures have been published nationally, and internationally. Many of the photos in this publication were taken by Joe.

Joe retired on April 19, 1976. His position, at this writing, has not been filled. The Photography Section was closed in June, 1976; thus ending an era.

Clarence C. Woodard
Fire Department Historian

Clarence C. Woodard has been concerned with the history of fire fighting since his high school days when he began a hobby of constructing miniature fire apparatus. Items from his collection were first used in 1932 when they were loaned to the Firemen's Fund Association to sell Field Day tickets at the Belle Isle Bridge. Through the years, items from his collection have been used for Fire Prevention exhibits at the Detroit Historical Museum, special Fire Prevention Week displays in public buildings, schools and other civic institutions.

Woodard has assembled more than one thousand photographs on this subject and the best of them have been selected for this book. Woodard has been a member of the Detroit Historical Society for many years, an honorary member of the Firemen's Fund Association and was appointed the first official historian of the Detroit Fire Department by the Board of Fire Commissioners in 1972.

Through the efforts of Woodard, Engine House 11 was placed on the State Register of Historical Places and application is now pending for its place on the National Register as a Fire Department Museum. Back in 1949, Woodard persuaded the Board of Fire Commissioners to donate two old pumpers, a 1922 Ahrens-Fox piston pumper, and a 1917 Seagrave to the Detroit Historical Museum. One of these units, the 1917 chain-drive Seagrave was turned over to the Box 42 Associates in the summer of 1977 and when operational will be joining the 1908 Ahrens steamer at the Engine 11 Museum.

Captain Jay W. Smith

Like many young lads born during or at the end of World War I, Jay W. Smith came through the very trying times of '29 and found himself the right age to be an active part of World War II. He served almost seven years in the Air Force, three years of which were in the South Pacific.

After returning in September, 1945 he joined the Detroit Fire Department. This would represent security for his family and a pension which is foremost in the minds of most everyone. It has been a rewarding experience for Captain Smith, both in serving the citizens of Detroit (most of that service in the 1st and 3rd Battalions) and gaining many fine friends along the way during his more than thirty-one years of service.

Approximately eighteen months ago Martin Snarsky, Acting Chief of Department asked him to assist on a committee to compile this historical record. The project has taken somewhat longer than anticipated, however the end results, as you see, are rewarding. The Committee hopes the results of its efforts in your behalf is a record which you will be as proud of as it is. The record of this Department over the past 100 years is partially yours and ours. You are members of one of the greatest Fire Departments in this country. You can and should be very proud. Together we, the Committee members, can only hope its greatness will continue over the years to come. It has been wonderful to have been a part of helping to put this historical record together.

Captain Joseph P. Boland

Joseph P. Boland was born, raised and educated on Detroit's East Side and graduated from St. Philip Neri High School in 1944. He served in the U.S. Navy during World War II primarily in the Pacific Theatre of Operations.

Honorably Discharged in 1946, Boland studied electrical engineering at the University of Detroit. After 2 years he decided that an engineering career was not to his liking and became a diesel truck mechanic for 3 years before joining the Detroit Fire Department in 1952. He served as Fire Fighter at Engine 9 and Ladder 19 before transferring to the Fire Marshal Division in 1954 and was assigned to the Public Instruction Section (then known as the Public Relations Section) where he has served since. He was promoted to Senior Fire Prevention Instructor (Captain) in 1972. Captain Boland and his wife Betty are proud of their 8 children.

Captain Boland was asked by Martin Snarsky, then Acting Chief of Department, to join with Captain Jay Smith in gathering material for a history book. They immediately enlisted the help of Mr. Clarence Woodard, Department Historian.

A Special Acknowledgement

My personal thanks to Mr. Clarence Woodard and Captain Jay W. Smith (retired) who worked so diligently and so persistently on the organizing and preparation of the contents of this publication. This book would not have become a reality without their efforts and we who read and enjoy its contents owe each of these men our gratitude.

Mr. Woodard, Detroit Fire Department Historian (by Fire Commission Action on October 31, 1972) submitted approximately 250 captioned pictures and almost 20,000 of his own words to the publisher. He has spent over 400 hours of his evenings and weekends, organizing, updating and rewriting his previously written material.

Captain Jay W. Smith retired during the preparation of this book, but while Captain of Engine 9, he accompanied the photographers to various locations and aided them while they made the portrait photographs of the Department members, by keeping records of who had or had not been photographed and by scheduling the most advantageous locations to which the fire companies responded for sittings. Captain Smith spent almost every leave day and extra leave day for 10 weeks (about 30 weekdays) aiding the photographers. A special thanks too, to Mrs. Woodard and Mrs. Smith who patiently tolerated this disruption to their homelife.

I believe I speak for the entire Department when I say THANK YOU CLARENCE AND JAY.

Most Sincerely,

Joseph P. Boland
Senior Fire Prevention Instructor
Fire Marshal Division

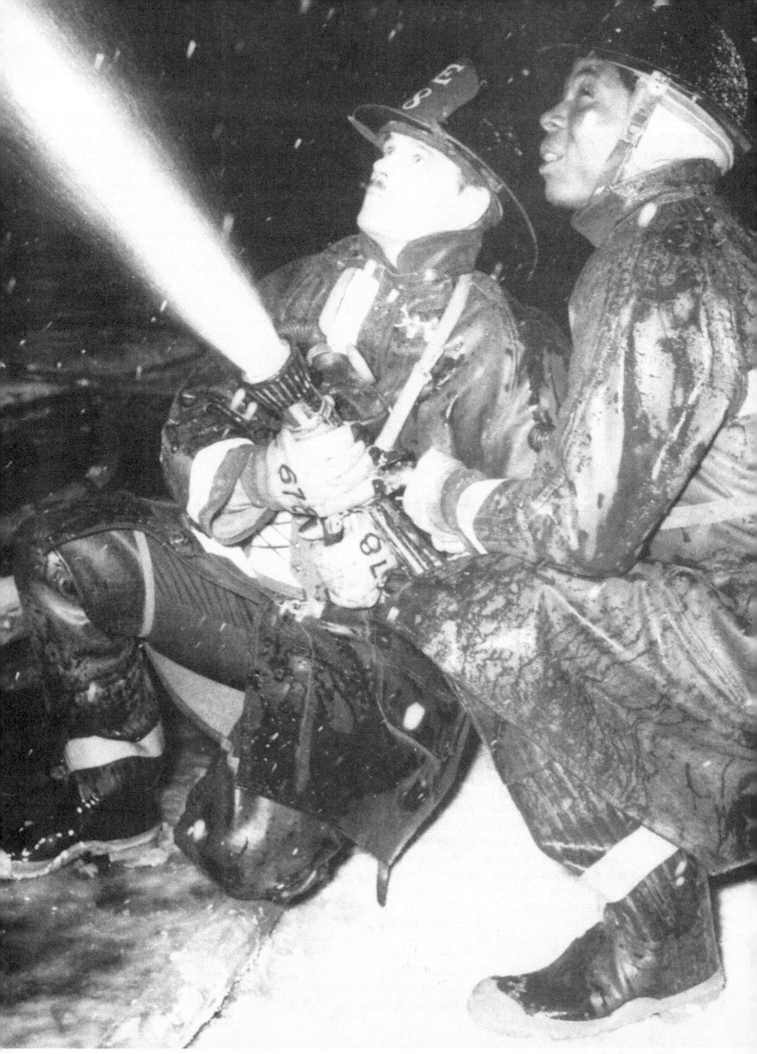

The Firemen's Creed

Who stands beside me when death brushes close?
Who's that at the nozzle? Who's pulling hose?
Are you my same color? Or pray in my pew?
Are you a Catholic, Protestant or Jew?

The walls on my chest, the smoke's got my eyes.
If I'm not reached soon, one more man dies.
Is that someone coming? I hope he's like me,
Of the same racial stock, the same old Country.

My mind must be drifting—the roof's caving in,
Firemen care not about Race, Creed or Skin,
Dunnigan or Levy, Morelli or Brown,
There's never been one to let a man down.

Who lugged me out after pushing through Hell?
Who helped me to live to see the next dawn?
Don't tell me his race and don't mention his creed.
Just say he's a fireman, for that's all I need.

What Is A Fireman?

He's the guy next door.

He's a man's man with the sharp memory of a little boy, who never got over the excitement of engines and sirens and smoke and danger.

He's a guy like you and with warts and worries and unfulfilled dreams.

Yet he stands taller than most of us.
He's a fireman.
He puts it all on the line when the bell rings.

A fireman is at once the most fortunate and the least fortunate of men.

He's a man who savors life because he has seen too much death. He's a gentle man because he has seen too much of the awesome power of violent forces out of control. He's a man responsive to a child's laughter because his arms have held too many small bodies that will never laugh again.

He's a man who appreciates the simple pleasures of life . . . hot coffee held in numbed, unbending fingers . . . the flush of fresh air pumping through smoke and fire convulsed lungs . . . a warm bed for bone and muscle compelled beyond feeling . . . the comraderie of brave men . . . the divine peace of selfless service and a job well done in the name of all men.

He doesn't wear buttons or wave flags or shout obscenities and when he marches, it is to honor a fallen comrade.

He doesn't preach the brotherhood of man,

He lives it.

- Acknowledgements -

The Book Committee is grateful for all the assistance and cooperation received from the individuals and organizations from the Commissioner's Office, down through the ranks of The Detroit Fire Department that made this publication possible.

PHOTOGRAPHY
Joseph A. Mancinelli - Official DFD Photographer (retired)
Barney W. Wasowicz - Acting DFD Photographer (retired)
City of Detroit, Dept. of Public Information
William Eisner - Fire Buff & Photographer
William Grimshaw - Fire Buff & Photographer
Walter McCall - Fire Buff & Photographer
The Detroit News
The Detroit Free Press

FIRE HISTORY
Ray A. Carle

DEPARTMENT HISTORY
Clarence C. Woodard

FIRE APPARATUS PHOTOS
American LaFrance Corp.
FWD-Seagrave Corp.
Mack Trucks, Inc.
Ward LaFrance Corp.
Clarence C. Woodard

BOOK COMMITTEE
Joseph P. Boland - Capt. Public Instruction Section
Jay W. Smith - Capt. Engine Co. 9 DFD (retired)
Clarence C. Woodard - DFD Historian

Turner®
PUBLISHING COMPANY

www.turnerpublishing.com

Library of Congress Control Number: 2005931265
ISBN: 978-1-68162-191-3
Limited Edition

Printed in the USA
CPSIA information can be obtained
at www.ICGtesting.com
JSHW060044150824
68134JS00031B/2628